Green Leaves

John Davey

Martin Luther Davey, Sr.

Martin Luther Davey, Jr.

Green Leaves

A History of
The Davey Tree Expert Company

BY

Robert E. Pfleger

The
Pequot
Press

Chester, Connecticut

Contents

Illustrations

Preface

In trying to analyze a company or appraise its success, there is always the temptation to look only at the balance sheet to determine the tangible assets and the rate of progress.

But the balance sheet fails to reveal the most important asset of all . . . people, and what motivated them. Behind the figures spilled out of a computer is always the story of human beings, their victories, their failures, their dedication, their sacrifices. Each of these plays a role in the making and building of a company and determining its character.

And so it is with the Davey Tree Expert Company. Its success is the victory of thousands of people brought about by the genius of three men whose leadership spanned a period of fifty years. A father, John Davey . . . inventor, dreamer, lover of all creation. A son, Martin L. Davey . . . the motivator, organizer, possessed of a deep and abiding respect for people. A grandson, Martin L. Davey, Jr. . . . a great respecter of the past, with a highly developed sense of the present and the future.

Each of these men was different. Each of them played a different role in bringing about the successful history of the company. However, even though there was a difference in their personalities, they held one thing in common . . . they established a spirit and a set of principles that are as alive today in the company as the oaks planted by John Davey nearly a hundred years ago.

John Davey, an English immigrant, created the science of tree surgery which ultimately resulted in a whole new industry and contributed immeasurably to the wealth and beauty of his adopted country. His son made it commercially available to tree owners across the nation.

His grandson made the business flourish and led it through its greatest and most dramatic period of growth. In the process they created opportunities for all kinds of people. John Davey would not have had it any other way, for this is what he believed the United States was all about . . . freedom of opportunity for all.

Author's Note

When I was offered the opportunity of writing a book about the first fifty years of the Davey Tree Expert Company, as a corporation, I welcomed it with a great deal of enthusiasm.

I had known the company for nearly thirty years as a client of the advertising agency with which I was associated for the major part of my business career. So I knew something of the company, its principles and objectives.

At first it appeared that the book would be a single chronicle of events about an interesting company and some of the people responsible for its success. But the events were like threads which soon wove themselves into a tapestry revealing a picture of the free-enterprise system . . . a system which created the greatest nation and the strongest economy the world has ever known.

Of course the system has produced many other successful companies and people. But what makes the Davey Tree Expert Company a classic study of free-enterprise is that it remains a privately-held, family-controlled business. It's not cluttered with mergers, buy-outs and sell-backs to confuse the picture. So its path to success is easy to follow.

As we explore that path, we soon discover that a good idea, by itself, is not enough for a successful venture. Then as we meet Martin L. Davey, we find that in the commercial aspects of the business he was as much a genius as his father, who created the science of tree surgery. The combined talents of these two resulted in a whole new industry.

While Martin L. Davey was an unusual man, we recognize in him the prototype of business people who capably manage the vast resources of American business. On the whole they are a hard-working, adaptable, creative group, who somehow have been able to guide 'their enterprises and keep them strong in face of wars, depressions, bureaucratic regulations and confiscatory taxation.

From time to time certain segments of our society take pleasure in attacking business. It appears that these critics are willing, almost anxious, to destroy the free-enterprise system. Someway, however, they would like to preserve the rewards and benefits the system has to offer.

Those critics might do well to examine John Davey's methods for saving trees and making plants flourish. Essentially what he discovered was that any kind of plant needs a favorable environment if it is to flourish, blossom and produce fruit. The same is true of business. It, too, needs a favorable environment if it is to grow and provide the fruit to keep our nation strong and give our people a better life.

—Robert E. Pfleger

Green Leaves

I "Do It Right or Not At All"

The science of tree surgery had a slow and laborious birth. It required nearly 50 years of study, observation and the insatiable curiosity of its inventor to bring it into being.

Although not apparent at the time, history seems to indicate that a great many of the things in the life of John Davey were directed toward the creation of the science of tree surgery. There were several times when he reached positions where he could have enjoyed a comfortable existence for as long as he lived, but some inner urge seemed to drive him on and on to the ultimate conclusion. From each of his experiences came knowledge and proof of methods that were ultimately brought together to establish the techniques and principles of a new science.

John Davey was born June 6th, 1846, on a farm which his father managed. It was located at Stawley in Somersetshire, England. From his father he inherited a passion for thoroughness and the satisfaction to be gained from a job well done.

Throughout his lifetime John Davey liked to relate an incident which occurred when he was four years old. He was watching his father plant potatoes and asked if he might plant one, too. The father cut a potato in half and then sent the youngster for a large iron spoon because the boy was too small to handle either a spade or a hoe. Then looking at young John he said, "Listen to me carefully. Do it right or not at all." Then he showed the boy how to plant the two pieces of potato and how to use the spoon to properly cover them. As the summer wore on, the boy lugged large pails of water for the plants. His father kept admonishing him, "Do it right or not at all."

Nigel Sweet (Grandson of man for whom John Davey worked) and Paul Davey at "Winkleigh"
Birthplace of John Davey located in the Parish of Stawley, near Wellington, Somersetshire, England.

This simple statement stayed with John Davey all of his life. It became a part of him. He lived it, practiced it and made it a part of the company he helped create almost 50 years later. In fact it became . . . and remains . . . the company's slogan.

His mother was responsible for another side of him. She was a woman of imagination and somewhat of a romanticist. Deeply religious as a devout member of The Church of England, she taught her family religion and to appreciate the beauties of nature which surrounded them, all the while encouraging them to be curious, to challenge and to learn. In the case of John Davey these seeds of wisdom fell on the fertile ground of an inquiring mind where they grew and flourished to become an integral part of him.

His mother died when he was thirteen years old. Because they had a large family the father placed the two older sons, one of whom was John, "out to service" with local farmers. During the next eight years John Davey learned the skills of a farmer. Their father received their pay until they were twenty-one. His thoroughness, and his willingness to give a hard day's work to his employer were recognized and appreciated. At eighteen he was made supervisor of cattle and all of the hired help. John Davey could have stopped here, assured of a slightly better life than his

4

peers, but when he became his own man at twenty-one he had other ideas.

He knew that there was little more he could learn about running and managing a farm and yet he recognized there was much more to learn about the plants and trees he admired so much. So, he decided to study horticulture and landscape gardening. He moved to Torquay in southern England, the seat of famous gardens and greenhouses. There he entered a six year apprenticeship where he learned greenhouse management, horticulture and finally floriculture in the thorough-going way of the Old World.

These were busy years for John Davey. It was during this time that he acquired a basic education. In his boyhood there were no schools for poor farmer boys, but in Torquay he met an educated man who taught him the alphabet. Armed with this knowledge, a new testament and a dictionary he very laboriously taught himself to read and write. Later he acquired a grammar and from it learned to put words together and use them correctly. About this time someone gave him a hymnal. This tiny library of four books was a great source of pride and provided him with many hours of satisfaction and comfort. It's doubtful that four books ever contributed more to the destiny of a person. The industry of the man was almost unbelievable. He spent ten to twelve hours a day at hard physical labor . . . then long hours into the night studying.

Along with his studies and his work he added still another activity. Through the kind auspices of his landlady he was introduced to Upton Vale Chapel where he met a congenial group of young men. Characteristically he plunged into the activities of the congregation full tilt. Certain evenings were set aside for social gatherings. Others were reserved for classes in religious education. On Sundays he and other young men of the congregation scoured the countryside for converts, preaching and conducting services wherever they found a welcome. This activity added another dimension to John Davey's character. He learned to be a persuasive speaker both with individuals, and with groups.

But this was a killing pace John Davey was following. It is no wonder that at the end of two years he became ill. He returned to the family farm and recovered in a relatively short time. Back he went to Torquay, this time determined to learn floriculture. Proof that he had regained his old energy and enthusiasm is indicated by the fact that he was put in charge of his employer's conservatory at the end of six months.

While the six years at Torquay certainly need to be labeled as a time of learning and maturing, this was also a time of opportunity for John Davey. The Rector of the church offered, on several occasions, to help him get located in a bank or other commercial establishment where the prospect of financial gain would be excellent. Others in the congregation offered to pay his tuition and his expenses for four years to Spurgeon College, the best seminary of the time. His employer was impressed with his work and his ability and wanted him to stay on, so offered him more money.

Any of these would have afforded a great deal more security and would have been a much smoother road than the one John Davey finally chose to travel. Money never was, nor, never did become the motivating force which drove him forward. It was ideas and the desire to understand the forces of nature that stimulated him.

The best insight into this side of his character is gained from his own words which he used to refuse each of these opportunities. To the kind friends who offered to send him to the Seminary he pointed out, "The Calvinistic tenets imposed by the college are not those I can subscribe to. I have a better opinion of the Heavenly Father than to believe that a certain few should be saved and that all the rest should be eternally damned equally for His glory."

About the commercial opportunities he had this to say, "I never had a head for figures and besides I had decided to work with soil all of my life." Of course he could have worked with soil in England and done very well. His own employer and several others with a need for a man of his character and expertise offered him employment; however, there was a new idea stirring within John Davey and soon became an obsession. All over Europe people were leaving for the New World. Finally, he decided that this was something he had to do also. So, after six eventful years he left the comfort and security of Torquay and turned his face toward a New World and a new life.

II   The New World

The fact that John Davey was willing to turn his back on security and move on to the unknown, provides another key to his character. He had supreme confidence in himself and his abilities. Besides some inner force seemed to drive him to find out what was behind the next mountain. America, and the freedom it offered, was the great adventure of the Nineteenth Century and John Davey knew he had to be a part of it.

He was twenty-seven years old when he migrated to the new world, landing in Castle Garden, New York, in the Spring of 1873. Shortly he went on to Warren, Ohio.

He could hardly have picked a worse time to migrate. The country was in a severe depression. In reminiscing about those times John Davey said, "Times grew steadily worse and unemployment increased. If a man was seen driving along with a load of bricks, men would run after him hoping to get a job laying those bricks. If a load of lumber went by, carpenters would flock after it hoping to get a job. Yet even in times like that I had more work than I could handle getting fifty cents more a day than other men received for the same kind of work. I think this was the result of learning the lesson my father taught me at the age of four, 'Do it right or not at all.'" One of his first jobs in the United States was as a janitor of a private school. Again his thirst for knowledge and an education came forward. He traded part of his labor for tuition. He learned Greek, Latin, Astronomy, and Botany as well as the standard courses offered. His favorite subjects naturally enough were the sciences, particularly those which dealt with plants and trees.

About this same time he acquired a greenhouse to help supplement his income. He also became active in a local church. Once more it was work, study and, on occasion, preaching.

Unfortunately the greenhouse was no financial success. John Davey was more interested in giving his customers something unusual and more than they expected, too often at the expense of his profit. The beauty of the flowers he grew and his skill with plants became well known and admired and this kind of compensation appeared to satisfy him more than money which he never seemed to understand or care much about.

During these years he became the espouser of causes. He favored women's suffrage as a way to abolish the local saloon and the tremendous influence it seemed to have in politics. But the cause to which he was most dedicated was the care and conservation of trees. He was appalled at the senseless waste of trees that went on in his adopted country. They were treated almost like an enemy that had to be destroyed. All they meant, to many, was cheap building material or an inexpensive source of fuel. Primeval forests were ripped out to provide farmland to grow food for an ever growing nation. As for sick trees the attitude was, "All plants die so what's so different about a tree?" Trees that were trimmed were made to look like hat racks by local "tree butchers." In spite of all this activity, he managed to include one more, which he often referred to as the "Fourth Milestone" in his life. He courted Bertha Reeves and married her in 1879. She was the daughter of the Reverend and Mrs. Harmon Reeves. He was Pastor of the Disciple Church of Warren.

The marriage was an ideal one. Bertha Davey, as the daughter of a poor minister, learned early how to make a little bit go a long way, skill she needed in her marriage because John Davey never acquired the knack of managing money. He was engrossed in ideas and his profession, and in trying to get others to join his crusade for the proper care of trees.

Shortly after the birth of their first child, a daughter they named Belle, the couple moved to Kent, Ohio, where John Davey received his first salaried job in the United States as caretaker of Standing Rock Cemetery. It was run down and suffering from years of neglect, filled with sadly abused trees and overgrown shrubbery. In a short time, under his skilled hands, what had once been a source of civic shame became one of pride. People came from far and near to marvel and admire John Davey's cemetery which he had transformed from a dilapidated graveyard to a beautiful memorial park. However, of more importance to him was the fact that he now had a laboratory where he could work without interference and demonstrate his revolutionary idea that trees could be saved by a practical curative process. In the doing he created a new sci-

DAVEY'S
Floral and Landscape Educator.

PUBLISHED MONTHLY BY JOHN DAVEY, FLORIST, WARREN, OHIO.

No. 2.]   WARREN, OHIO, NOVEMBER, 1878.   [Price 25 cents a Year

Important as religious and political discussions may be, in their place, they will not be allowed in these columns.

"DESPISE NOT THE DAY OF SMALL THINGS."

Though, at its birth, this paper is small, I hope to enlarge it step by step; treating only of Floriculture, Horticulture, Farming, Art and Science; designed, on the whole, to elevate and refine taste, and thus do its part in blessing humanity.

This issue will be considered the November number.

Have been using one issue hitherto as a specimen number until I have a fair list of subscribers.

. The article, "Lucky" and "Unlucky Farmer," will not appear in this issue, as another article takes its place.

This paper is designed to appear on or about the 1st of every month, and will contain instruction for that month.

All who have become entitled to this paper by purchasing plants, and all who have subscribed will be considered as October subscribers, and will receive the paper till the same month, 1879.

As there will be no need of a great amount of instruction on plant culture, during the winter months, I shall treat largely on the method of English farming, and also explain the manner of English frugal living.

I offer a new honeysuckle, "Captain Moisey." It is named after an English gentleman on whose estate the seed was produced. The exterior of the flower is a beautiful shade of pink; interior, yellow. It is very fragrant and perfectly hardy. Small plants, 50c. It will be sent by mail, postage prepaid, on receipt of price. All who purchase it will be entitled to the EDUCATOR for one year. It should be planted before hard frost, as it will get an advantage in starting in spring.

Dahlias must now be lifted from the open ground. Cut off their branches, leaving three or four inches of the stalk. Shake all the earth carefully from the roots. Lay them out in the open sun by day, for a while, so as to dry them well. Then if convenient, place them in dry earth in a vessel in which you can start them. If not desirous to start them early in spring, place them away in a dry cellar, in boxes of fine dry earth or sand.

Gladiolus should now be lifted. Very likely the stalks of those that were planted late are still green. Lay such in the sun by day, until somewhat dried. The bulbs will mature better by allowing the stalks to remain on till dry. Then cut off stalks and lay in cellar or closet, in a dry place, away from frost. You can generally keep Gladiolus and Dahlias where you can safely winter potatoes.

A great many enquire for roses for winter blossoming. Of course this being "The Queen of Flowers," it is very much to be desired; but let me say, there is but one course which will insure success in its blooming well in winter, or rather, spring. Such plants as are desired for "Winter blooming," should be grown in pots in summer. This partially checks their growth. In the latter part of summer turn them out of the pots, wash the earth carefully from the roots, and replace in a suitable size pot, in good potting soil. Let them get well rooted in Fall, then set them in a dry place in the cellar, and keep dry. About the first of February place them in a cool sitting room, where it is just kept from freezing. Water lightly. They will thus start with the progress of spring and will continue to bloom till hot weather.

Watering Pot Plants.

"How often must I water?" "How much water do pot plants require?" are the kind of questions continually asked. About the only correct answer I know, is, water whenever they need it; if it is ten times a day or once a month. The best way to inform a person how often to water, is to give him ideas when a plant needs water. In the first place, always get a flower-pot sufficiently large for the plant which is to be put in it. Secondly, be sure the pot is clean, and always keep it clean. Thirdly, never use a glazed or a painted pot. Painting or glazing always stops the pores, and the drainage thus being stopped, the majority of people will blunder at some time, by giving too much water and will thus sour the earth and rot off the rootlets. The supply thus cut off from the plant, the leaves turn yellow and drop from the branches. There is scarcely ever any danger of that kind, where the common earthenware pot is used and kept clean, such a vessel is a perfect drainage in itself. Always see that the hole for drainage, in the bottom, is large enough; if it is too small, enlarge it. Place on this hole, pebble stones or broken pieces of flower pots to prevent its being choked with earth. Pot your plant in suitable soil, and water well to settle and embed the earth around the fibres; place in a shady situation and not water for three or four days, only sprinkle the leaves to keep them fresh. This cessation of watering gives the fibres a chance to make a fresh hold in the soil. Thousands upon thousands of plants are killed yearly, from a continuous watering after potting or re-potting; the rootlets become rotten before they have a chance to work in the new soil. From this point you may have two

ence . . . tree surgery. During this time he developed many mechanical and scientific principles that have become basic in the practice of tree surgery. After several years John Davey left this position because, as he put it, "I don't want to spend any more time in a graveyard while I'm alive."

While people saw at Standing Rock what the new science could do in saving trees, they were slow to accept the idea, regarding it for the most part as something that was not necessary. However, a few thought

THE RESTORATION BAND *of* AMERICA

NATIONAL HEADQUARTERS : KENT, OHIO

===== *Presenting* =====

"THE SALVATION OF OUR TREES AND BIRDS"

AN ILLUSTRATED LECTURE BY JOHN DAVEY

THE BOARD OF TRADE
WILLIAMSPORT, PA.

Nov. 26, 1912.

The splendid lecture on "The Salvation of Our Trees and Birds," recently given before the members of this Board by Mr. John Davey, was one of the most interesting and instructive ever given in this city. It has served to stimulate a renewed interest in the care of our trees, and also the birds which are the protectors of the trees, and I am sure will result in much good to our city.

We heartily commend this lecture to all Boards of Trade and civic bodies.

(Signed) DON. M. LARRABEE,
Mgr. Williamsport Board of Trade.

PRESIDENT'S OFFICE
HIRAM COLLEGE
HIRAM, OHIO

Nov. 26th, 1912.

Mr. John Davey, Kent, Ohio.

My Dear Mr. Davey:

The life value of your lectures before our students grows upon me. It is time that young men should appreciate the unity and interdependence of the entire world of life. You have made us all feel a new kinship with the trees and birds and our consequent interdependence. You have a message which should be brought home to the hearts of all the youth of our land.

Sincerely yours,
(Signed) MINER LEE BATES,
President.

JOHN DAVEY
"FATHER OF TREE SURGERY"

5 — 21 — /13.

Dear Mrs. Ratliff:

O. K. Will be our after a few weeks. not quite time to trim hedge. Don't let any one touch it. Best wishes to all

Davey

John Davey

Belle	Wellington	Martin
Davey	Davey	Luther
Carson		Davey, Sr.

enough of it that he developed a small local following and he became the town's "tree man." To supplement his income, he acquired a greenhouse and a small plot of ground where he planned to grow and sell produce.

In the meantime, he became a pamphleteer and lecturer. Always the student, always alert to current affairs, his subjects ranged far and wide. He lectured and wrote about politics, religion, the Kaiser, communism, birds, child care, farm problems and always carried on a continuing crusade to enlist support for the proper care and conservation of trees.

He was well accepted as a lecturer. As he progressed he used to

11

illustrate his talks with slides. When his five children became old enough several of them would go along to handle props or to add variety to the program by giving recitations. Often, these were poems written by John Davey.

But none of these activities helped solve the economic facts of life to any great extent. The pamphlets sold for a nickel which barely paid for the paper they were printed on. The lectures provided little more. In this whole arena John Davey was at his very best. These activities provided him with a creative outlet that was like food and drink to his spirit. They also provided a rather positive effect as well. He became well known and gradually people began to say, "There might be something to what that fellow from Kent tells us about trees." But that took a long time to come about, with plenty of struggle in between.

III We Meet
Martin Luther Davey

John Davey's principal battle was with money. A man of no vices, talented, hard-working, willing and able to do many things, he had a difficult time providing for his family. Possessed of a variety of skills, the ability to hold on to money was not one of them.

In his family there were seven children. Five of them, Belle, Wellington, Martin, Jim and Paul, grew to maturity. They knew what it was like to be poor, but poverty never warped their spirits or destroyed their sense of values. They were naturally bright and were also good students. Their mother saw to that. Proud and sensitive, they felt the shame of poverty in a way their father, never did. They were subjected to the judgment of those whose criterion of success was a tangible display of wealth.

In one way, they were the wealthiest family in town. They were constantly exposed to an exciting world of ideas, about all kinds of subjects. They had excellent religious training and practiced it and lived it by showing their love and respect for each other, willing always to make personal sacrifices for the benefit of the family as a whole. These were valuable assets . . . the kind that are not for sale.

It was out of this crucible that the second son, Martin L., emerged. Tempered by the fires of adversity, he was to play an important role in the family fortunes and to serve his country as mayor, congressman and governor. His career finally took him far beyond those whose slights to him and his family in the years of his youth stung and scarred like a whiplash. But first he had some learning and growing-up to do. Martin L. was always a salesman and a leader, talents which became apparent at an early age. One of his first enterprises was to prepare and sell horseradish. He established a regular route and the five cents he made on each jar went into the family "kitty." Along with the profit, he learned how to make friends of his customers. This was easy for him because he had a warm personality and a genuine liking for people, attributes that marked his character as long as he lived.

He also worked in the fields with his brothers to help raise the crops which were sold to the people in town (when enough was "put down" for the family's winter food supply). While the summer wore on the Davey menage literally buzzed like a beehive with activity. When crops were harvested the wagon was loaded and the boys would go along with their father to help sell the produce. As they rumbled along in the horse-drawn wagon Father John took the opportunity to tell them about one or another of the many subjects about which he was so knowledgeable. It might be Astronomy, plants, or the part a leaf played in the life of a tree. Whatever it was, he made the facts as exciting as any fairy tale written by the brothers Grimm. Sometimes, just for the pure joy of being alive, they would all burst into song, alerting their customers that they were on the way long before they got to them.

There was never a king who knew greater pleasure than the times John Davey and his boys spent together. These were moments to be remembered and treasured forever.

Time and again throughout his life Martin L. used his tremendous skill as a salesman to solve a wide variety of problems. But this ability was never used to better advantage than the time he put it to work in behalf of his sister Belle. She was about to graduate from High School at the head of her class. But there was no money available to buy her a new dress for the occasion. This was indeed a crisis and a tragedy in a young girl's life. Martin went about solving it by first persuading his father to give him a huge bed of pansies that were of unusual beauty and quality. These he sold door-to-door for premium prices, making enough to buy not only a new dress for Belle, but a new hat for his mother . . . and his own first pair of long pants. This was characteristic of Martin all of his life, to move in . . . take charge . . . and solve the problem. This incident also revealed his sensitivity for the feelings of others and how he sympathized with them.

In the meantime, Martin broadened his sphere of activity. He and his brother-in-law, Harmon Carson, were selling aluminum combs in Cleveland. It was hard but profitable work and helped to pay his way through High School. During the summers he continued to help on the

(L to R) Unknown, Bertha Davey (in rocking chair), John Davey,
Wellington Davey, Harmon Carson (husband of Belle Davey),
Martin L. Davey, unknown, Belle Carson Davey (at
corner of porch), on lawn Paul H. Davey,
James A. G. Davey.

family farm which had been expanded to include some muck land John
Davey bought to go into the commercial production of celery and onions.

Then like many other young men of a similar age, Martin started to
think about a career. During the time he was turning the problem over
in his mind he attended a County Fair and heard William Jennings
Bryan give his famous "Cross of Gold" speech, and it was then he re-
solved that by the proper use of words, voice, and skill he would turn his
life work into something practical.

In the next few years, after graduating from Kent High School, his
activities were centered in nearby Cleveland. It appeared that he was
well on the road to success. As a result he was experiencing a growth of
confidence in himself. For some reason, probably due to poverty in his
childhood, he had harbored the feeling that he was not quite as good as
many others. In trying to explain this later in his life he said, "In Kent

15

there were many people who were very kind to me. However, there were some who subjected me to gibes and ridicule, and these had their effect. Those early years in Cleveland taught me that people were willing to accept me for myself." While the acceptance gave him confidence the slights seemed to be the spur and the whip which drove him on to the determination to show the doubters, and the whole world, what he could do. While discovering himself, Martin was accumulating a fund of practical knowledge that he found useful all of his life. An older man, who had taken an interest in him, gave him a valuable piece of advice. He cautioned Martin never to forget the "little man." He put it this way, "Those who are popular accept your attentions as a matter of fact and seldom appreciate it. Notice the neglected and they will sing your praises everywhere." This was easy for him to practice with sincerity because he had an empathy with the neglected. For too long he had felt he was one of them.

It was during these years that he accepted a position in Cleveland as a salesman for the Oliver Typewriter Company, this job paid ten dollars a week plus commission. He was soon earning two-hundred dollars a month, a very substantial income in that day and age, and far more

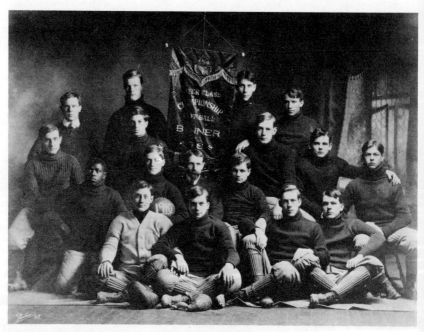

Oberlin Football Team of 1906. Martin L. Davey circle.

than others on the staff. He credited a large part of his success in this endeavor to his early training which taught him the value of hard work. While other salesmen sat around the office dreaming about the next sale, he was out in the territory calling on customers and persuading them to buy the machines he had to offer.

Although he was doing quite well financially, he made yet another discovery about himself. Money, for itself, and to the exclusion of all else, would never be his goal. Martin, like his father and brothers, was highly creative and liked stimulating ideas. Some of this he satisfied by reading and exploring the classics. It was expressed in another way as well. All of his life people stimulated him and he had an inherent ability to use his creative power to motivate people and lead them to heights they never dreamed possible.

In spite of the success he was enjoying, Martin decided he wanted to further his education. So he enrolled in Oberlin College at Oberlin, Ohio, and with typical Davey energy and enthusiasm, he was soon playing football and running on the track team. He also opened a haberdashery shop on campus. Scholastically he was also one of three leaders of his class. But during these college years a number of events were taking place at home. Many of them he played an important part in bringing about. Little did he know at the time how they were to change and shape his life.

IV   The Tree Doctor

The Davey tree care work was expanding, resulting from the evidence that existed around Kent and Warren, Ohio, that trees could be saved and made to flourish with proper attention. The business was gradually growing and finally reached the point where there was enough work to keep Father John and two of his sons busy. Wellington, the oldest, joined his father in 1900. Jim, the other son, became associated with his father and brother in 1904. The three of them offered tree care and landscaping service.

However, a much more important event was taking place. Father John let it be known that he was writing a book on tree care. He was convinced that people really liked trees and neglected them only because of sheer ignorance, so he would show them the way. At first this caused no stir, for after all he was always writing something. But soon the whole family got caught up in the excitement. At one point Father John asked Martin to suggest a title for the book, but before he could offer one, Father John announced that it would be called "The Tree Doctor." It was the first serious work concerned with shade trees. Until John Davey's effort, tree literature was confined principally to fruit trees.

While the "Tree Doctor" was a handbook for those who had an interest in protecting and promoting the growth and health of plants and trees, it did something else as well.

The book demonstrated that John Davey's methods for "doctoring trees" were based on sound scientific methods and observation and did not result from green-thumb luck. In the book he discussed the importance of leaves, the tree's root system, the cell structure, the cambium, the

How a tree cavity is located.

flow of sap, and their nutritional needs. Then he pointed out the relationships these elements had to each other and why they had to be kept in precise balance if a tree was to remain healthy.

From one of his observations came the development of cavity filling, considered to be one of the most dramatic operations in the science of tree surgery.

A study of the cross sections of hollow trees led to the discovery that the callus, which nature had intended to cover the wound, had instead bent inward in the absence of a supporting surface, forming spirals on the edge of the cavity on either side of the opening. After years of experimentation, John Davey developed a sophisticated method of filling the hollow tree cavities with concrete, which accomplished the purpose of providing a supporting surface for the callus.

However, a cavity filling required much more than dumping some concrete into a hole in a tree. As a matter of fact it demanded a great deal of skill and knowledge to do it properly. Filling a cavity in a tree is very similar to the way a dentist fills a tooth.

To repair a cavity great care must be taken to protect the delicate edges of the bark, sap-wood and cambium and it needs to be done in such a way that the opening conforms to the normal flow of sap. The decay needs to be traced to its furtherest extent and completely removed. The walls of the cavity must be carved in such a manner that the filling will be retained after it is in place.

As soon as the cavity is opened, the bark edges are immediately protected by a special coating to prevent drying out of the delicate living tissue lying directly underneath. After the cavity is carved, it is carefully disinfected to destroy any and all remaining trace of decay fungus. After the disinfectant is dry, a special waterproofing material is applied to seal the wood from further exposure to moisture and fungous growth.

Just inside the cavity, a series of "watershed grooves," are carved with the utmost care and connected to a copper tube at the bottom of the cavity to drain off moisture.

If the cavity is of sizeable proportions, in relation to the size of the tree, it is sometimes necessary to provide mechanical support by installing a system of steel bracing.

After all of these things are done, the cavity is ready for filling. The concrete is applied in sections, each section separated from the next by three-ply tarpaper. The sections are contoured on either end to resemble the nature and shape of the human spine. This permits the tree to sway fully in the wind without cracking the concrete filling. The same tech-

21

Tree surgeons engaged in an unusual operation. The black oak and tulip had practically grown together at their bases so that they appeared to be different trees springing from the same trunk. Decay set in at the point of juncture and elsewhere, necessitating the operation.

niques discovered in those early days are still used today when tree cavities are treated.

Another of John Davey's observations reported in his book was the proper trimming of limbs from a tree. He found that, if a limb was cut off leaving a stub, it would eventually rot at that spot leaving a hole in the tree. His method was to cut the limb off at the shoulder, then paint the cut. In this way the cambium layer would grow over the wound and the tree would heal. In the early days of tree care, removal of larger limbs called for the cuts to be covered with a zinc cap. Later, a special liquid coating called Daveyite was formulated which provided protection for tree cuts from moisture and promoted healing.

Father John also devised a method to support structurally weak trees with a system of chains and rods without destroying the beauty or sym metry of the tree. The efficiency of this system has been proved by the many trees, standing today, which were protected by rods and chains installed nearly a century ago.

His work in agriculture taught him that trees are just large plants that need great quantities of food and moisture. Most shade trees living on lawns are deprived of their proper supply of water and decaying vegetation which would enable them to flourish in the forest. Again, John Davey devised methods for feeding and watering trees. This sometimes required an intricate system of tiling.

The tile were laid horizontally on a two percent grade. The system carried off excess water while at the same time it enabled trees to get the proper amount of moisture and air. It also provided a means of applying fertilizer. The method was particularly valuable in city locations where tree roots extended under pavements or sidewalks.

Another, and much more common method of applying fertilizer to trees, consisted of punching a series of holes over the entire root area to the edge of the drip line and applying either a liquid or solid fertilizer.

John Davey had little notion about the forces his book would unleash. He had some vague idea that it might produce a profit but that was the most he hoped for. He was convinced that everyone shared his enthusiasm for trees and plants and would pay to get sound information about their proper care. However, as is often the case, he was unable to find a publisher for his work. In spite of the fact that it was unique, and did offer tree owners and plant lovers valuable knowledge available in no other form, there was a great doubt on the part of the firms he approached that there would be any kind of sale for a book like "The Tree Doctor."

Finally, in desperation, he decided to publish it himself. This was a momentous decision requiring him to go into debt for $7,000—a lot of money in those days and especially to a man of his means. But John Davey never lacked confidence in a course of action he had decided on, and he never went part way. It was always, "Do it right or not at all." So finally, in 1901, "The Tree Doctor," was exposed to public view.

During the first year he was encouraged by the sales made throughout Northern Ohio book stores. Its greatest sales, however, came principally from the Hudson Valley and in Boston, the location of many large estates.

Again, Martin, the family sales expert, was called into service. He was given the assignment of selling the book on commission of 50 cents per copy. About half the sales during the first year were credited to his

OFFICE OF

JOHN DAVEY

Author of

"The Tree Doctor"

KENT, OHIO

The accompanying cut shows a gang of Young "Tree Doctors," as they are commonly called.

We employ no man who uses alcoholic drinks or tobacco in any form. This is not so much from a temperance "Hobby," as from a NECESSITY. The man who uses these things, we have found, has "shaky nerves" and often declines to ascend the heights necessary to go.

All the men are young, hence ACTIVE; they are all thoroughly drilled; they are intelligent and have studied trees physiologically, just the same as a student would to enter the practice of SURGERY. They are furnished with a full line of tools, belts, guard ropes and ladders, specially constructed to be carried into the tops of high trees.

We undertake no work by "Contract," for the reason that we have learned that there is no possible way of telling what we are going to run into. Nor do we undertake anything where the owner desires "just a little light trimming." We leave all such work for the "Tree Butchers" who have already ruined millions of trees. We have but one rule in such matters, i. e., if we undertake any work, IT MUST BE DONE RIGHT, regardless of cost. However, for all work put in our charge we pledge faithful service. Our motto is "GOOD MEN AND GOOD WAGES."

For the men in general we charge $3 a day for a 9-hour day. For the foreman, $5 a day is charged. All the men sign a contract of a few simple rules, among which is, for the season, not to form "Unions" or any organization that would stop or impede the work.

To the above costs of work, all materials used on trees, such as paints, bolts, etc., must be paid for by owner of trees.

To the foregoing expenses of work, must be added 15 per cent. on the bill of a job of work, to cover the cost of my inspecting trees, superintending work, etc. For example, if it costs $10 to fix a tree or trees, $1.50 is added for my own personal services; if the cost be $100, $15 is added, etc. Work at very long distances might necessitate a greater charge for my own personal services, concerning which an understanding can be had before work commences.

I have prepared this circular to do away with delays in exchanging letters on the subject.

Any work entrusted to me will be executed with honor.

As references concerning the character of our work I will give: Messrs. Paul E. Werner, C. C. Goodrich, R. P. Marvin, and J. T. Johnson, of Akron, O.; Messrs. R. A. Harman, and S. L. Severance, of the Park-Euclid National Bank, Cleveland, O.; Mr. Frank W. Hart, Cleveland, O.; Messrs. J. E. French, and W. H. Silverthorn, of New York City.

Kindly address me at Kent, O.

Most respectfully,

JOHN DAVEY.

efforts. In Warren, Ohio, alone he sold books to about twenty-five percent of the families living there.

There appeared to be two classes of readers. One, the man with one or two trees who used the book as a text to guide him in properly caring for them. The other, which appeared to be a much larger group, were wealthy people who owned large estates interested in protecting and saving the trees on their property. While the book went into great detail in explaining how to treat trees, and the methods and results were profusely illustrated with photographs, some estate owners found their own people reluctant to do the work. Others, with magnificent specimen trees, were unwilling to trust them to people without experience. As a consequence, many of these owners contacted John Davey and asked for his assistance.

Another possible explanation for the interest in the book was that public officials and their constituents were becoming increasingly aware that the natural beauty of the United States needed to be conserved for future generations. John Davey's dream was starting to take on substance.

One of the important effects of the book was in winning the support of influential people to join John Davey's crusade to save and properly care for trees. One of these was J. Horace McFarland of Harrisburg, Pennsylvania. He was the owner of a large printing business but, more importantly from the standpoint of John Davey, he was President of the American Civic Association, an organization devoted to the improvement of Public Affairs. McFarland was influential with people at various levels of government, educators and others in positions of leadership.

He was very much impressed with John Davey's knowledge and integrity. In effect, he became his unofficial advisor and Public Relations man. McFarland arranged invitations for nature talks, diagnostic clinics, and helped make other contacts, all of which brought new business, new acceptance and new fame to John Davey. Another powerful ally was George Eastman of Kodak fame. He was a great admirer of John Davey and his new science of tree surgery, and since John Davey was an avid user of a camera, the two found much in common.

In the Fall of 1908 Mr. Eastman arranged a date for John Davey to present a lecture to the wealthiest and most prominent citizens of Rochester, New York. So many assignments came out of the meeting that all of the available Davey men in the area were swamped with work.

The book also caused a controversy in the city of Cleveland the "Forest City." In one of the chapters, John Davey charged that officials there were guilty of what amounted to criminal neglect of the city's shade trees, because so many of them were dying. A newspaper grabbed the issue and soon it was raging throughout the city. Officials claimed that smoke from factories was destroying the trees. Davey argued that they were dying because of lack of soil around the roots and that heavy sod was cutting off their food and water supply. People rallied around the stand he took with the result that the city petitioned the State Legislature to permit the establishment of a Division of Forestry to provide "Davey Type" care for the trees. This was done, and in a later edition of his book, John Davey complimented the Cleveland officials for their successful course of action which did indeed save the trees.

From all of this interest and discussion, it slowly began to dawn on John Davey that his book was creating a result that he had never contemplated. He had originally assumed that inquiries from the book could be easily handled by him and his boys. He began to realize this was not to be the case and that he was going to be forced to organize for something much bigger than anything he had ever imagined. The demand for Davey Tree Service was expanding throughout Ohio and into Pennsylvania, New York, Washington, D. C., and even into Canada in cities like Toronto and Ottawa.

To meet this growing demand, and to supply the crews with trained manpower, he and his son, Wellington, organized the Davey School of Practical Forestry to teach men how to minister to ailing trees. While this activity helped to solve one part of the problem there were other pressures that were building up because of an expanding business. There was a great deal of tree work to be done in the Cleveland and Pittsburgh areas and in the Hudson Valley, making it very difficult for John Davey to cover all of the bases.

In the Spring of 1906 he wrote a letter to Martin, who was at Oberlin College telling him that he was greatly needed. He asked him to go east for the summer to look after the business there and to take over the sales work in that area. Because of the urgency expressed in this letter, Martin agreed. Jim Davey was also sent east and was put in charge of the field crews. Martin secured permission from his father to invite several of his Oberlin classmates to join him. In addition, John Davey arranged for some of the students from Massachusetts Agriculture College, who had previously worked for him, to join the crews working under Jim Davey's direction. They made high type working crews.

One of the assignments was on the W. B. Dickerman estate, located in Mamaroneck, New York. The year before, Dickerman, a man of great wealth and influence, had called upon John Davey to save a giant elm.

The tree was a beautiful specimen and Mr. Dickerman was very proud of it.

The great elm stood near a fence line and the soil beneath it on one side was heavy and the grass roots very deep. On the other side, the soil was cultivated. But the great tree was rather sad looking. It seemed to be dying from root to crest . . . but only on one side. The other side, where the soil had been cultivated beneath, the tree was green and healthy.

John Davey went about treating the tree by first digging a semi-circular trench about three feet wide and three feet deep on the sodded side of the fence and forty feet out from the base of the elm. At that point, he cut off all but the largest roots and filled the trench with well-rotted manure which he worked into the soil. Next he dug out all of the sod between the trench and the tree. In this space, he worked several wagon loads of manure into the soil.

By the next year the tree was beautiful and green on all sides. John Davey pointed out that the only reason for the sad condition the tree had been in, was due to the thick sod on the one side that prevented natural nutrients and moisture from reaching the roots; while on the other side, where the earth had been cultivated and regularly fertilized, the tree remained strong and healthy.

This dramatic demonstration greatly pleased Mr. Dickerman. As a result he became very interested in the Daveys and tried to help by introducing and recommending them to his friends and neighbors, who did use their service to a limited degree.

Even with this help there were not enough regular assignments to keep the crews constantly busy. This meant that Martin had to pour himself into his work. He walked many miles a day in search of business. He was finding that it was somewhat more difficult than he originally thought it would be to get all the orders he wanted and needed. He was offering a new service so he had to sell the idea and philosophy of tree care. After Martin did that, he had to convince the prospect that *his* trees needed care. Finally, after several weeks of back breaking efforts, he got a big break. He learned of an oil man of great wealth by the name of Henry M. Flagler one of the original Standard Oil men, who owned a large and beautiful estate on Orienta Point along the shore of Long Island Sound, just off Mamaroneck. Martin arranged for an opportunity to walk through the grounds and study the trees very carefully. He found a number of them in serious need of attention. His next step was to arrange for an appointment with Mr. Flagler and persuade him of the need for having the work done. The result was the largest order in the fledgling history of Davey Service. It was the key that unlocked the door to many other sales. By early fall the Davey operations had expanded to the western side of the county, in the vicinity of Tarrytown, on the banks of the Hudson.

While the Flagler deal was of the utmost importance, it did something else as well. It caused Martin to lay down a step-by-step procedure for selling his service. The first step was to sell the concept of tree care and then translate that into terms of the prospect's own trees. When that was done, it was time to present the idea that only Davey could do the work in a proper manner.

There was still another problem which he had to overcome. The kind of men he was dealing with, particularly in Westchester, demanded a specific understanding about which trees were to be treated and how much it would cost. This led Martin to the first step toward the solution of a problem that had been nagging his father ever since the business had expanded beyond the environs of Kent, Ohio. The answer was the development of an estimating procedure based on time needed to do a

Martin L. Davey in 1904

Courting days
Martin L. Davey and
Berenice Chrisman

job. The estimate became a vital part of every transaction, and remains so to this day. The document is not only important to the client and Davey, but to the people charged with the responsibility for doing the work.

The victories of that summer and fall were once again proof of Martin's power of persuasion. The development of the estimate demonstrated he had a very practical side as well.

As the vacation period was ending and there was enough business to keep the crews busy until the cold weather would set in and prevent further work, Martin decided to return to college.

When Martin returned home from Oberlin for the Easter vacation, in the spring of 1907, his father pleaded with him to stay out of school until fall when, he assured him, he could return. He offered him a full partnership and a free hand to manage the Eastern business according to his judgment and without interference. This was an offer too good to refuse, so Martin accepted, recognizing this was an unusual opportunity for a young man approaching his twenty-third birthday.

There was another big event which took place in Martin's life during this year of 1907. He married Berenice Chrisman of Kent. The couple had three children; Evangeline, later Mrs. Alexander M. Smith, Mary Berenice who died in childhood and Martin L., Jr.

This ended Martin's dream of a college education and started him down the road which would enable him to reach another goal, "To Show the World," and eventually he did. In a very real sense it was another direct effect of John Davey's brainchild, "The Tree Doctor."

V Success in
the Hudson Valley

Martin's lofty status as a full-fledged partner in the Eastern business sounded more impressive than it really was at the time. A cynical person might have asked, "A partner in what?". The business was debt ridden to the extent of $25,000. Further, it lacked any semblance of an organization. While his agreement called for him to share in the profits, there were little or none to share. Tree surgery was not only a new business, it was a new industry which made it impossible to "borrow" ideas from others successfully engaged in a similar enterprise.

But it is obvious that Martin recognized a potential, which many with less vision failed to see. There were a number of assets, and the book "The Tree Doctor" was one of the most important of these. It synthesized nearly fifty years of philosophy, discovery and practical application of methods which made up the science of Tree Surgery. It was receiving favorable reviews, drawing attention to John Davey's work and helping to make him famous. There was a sizeable demand for the services and it was growing with a list of prestigious clients that would be the envy of any business, new or old. It included names like Dickerman, Islein, Flagler, Archbold, Rockefeller—men who were industrial and financial leaders of the country. Martin's experience proved to him that tree care could be sold to a demanding and critical client. For whatever might be said of the men he dealt with there, they were hard-nosed when it came to a business deal. They not only bought the service, but were willing to endorse and recommend it to others—something they would never do unless they were completely satisfied, for they were not the kind to permit their names to be used or bandied about by just anyone.

Martin L. Davey driving
a Maxwell Runabout.

One of his first actions after rejoining the company, in the spring of 1907, was to establish an office in an old house which he rented on the corner of Broadway and Main Street in Tarrytown, New York. Soon Martin was caught up in a wide variety of details. In addition to being a salesman and sales manager, he had to keep the books, send out the bills, pay the men, collect the accounts, provide the necessary tools and materials, and hire men and see to it they were trained.

It was about this same time he made another decision. He recognized that his progress would be greatly impeded unless he could get around the territory at a faster pace. So he bought a used two-cylinder Maxwell automobile, which incidentally was manufactured in Tarrytown. The car was bought with money which he had to borrow. But he reasoned he could produce enough additional business to make it a worthwhile investment. He soon learned that the upkeep of the car was an item of considerable expense, but it did serve an important function in the business.

By 1908 the business had expanded up the Hudson to the vicinity of Poughkeepsie and over into Western Connecticut, as well as New Jersey. The operation had grown to include three salesmen in addition to Martin.

It was during this time that he persuaded his brother Jim to become a salesman and he was a good one. But he had one fault, he wouldn't make out an expense account. After a great deal of nagging, Martin finally estimated his expenses at the end of a year and paid him a lump sum.

What Martin really stepped into was a mob action where things were happening pell mell with little relationship between cause and effect. What he did was form an organized army to help him achieve victory.

The success Martin was having in the East lead him to the conclusion that the same business building technique could be applied to a much larger area.

As he thought about this, he felt that the headquarters of the business should be established in Kent, Ohio. He reasoned that this location was near the center of the territory in which they wanted to operate, so Martin's assumption was that it would be less expensive and much more convenient to operate there. During the time Tarrytown was the center of operations, the family maintained a residence in Kent. So it meant that every Spring they had to move, lock, stock and baggage east and then move back again in the Fall. So the decision was made. On December 1, 1908 Martin established headquarters in Kent, Ohio.

Later Martin admitted that the move was somewhat premature. Hindsight indicated that it might have been much more advantageous to have maintained the base of operations in the east and expand westward. The move spread the available manpower too thin and as a result, they were trying to cover too much territory with a limited force. Expenses increased, including much heavier transportation costs. But the die was cast and it was only after the actual experience in the new location that the decision could be properly evaluated. By then it was much too late to do anything about it.

At this time Father John was taking a less active role in the business, devoting himself largely to lecture work and the writing of additional books. This included a revised and enlarged edition of "The Tree Doctor" and "Davey's Primer on Trees and Birds," a small book intended for children. In addition he published a brochure called "A New Era in Tree Growing" which was used as a sales promotion piece.

As more and more of the responsibility of running the business fell on Martin's shoulders, he started to plan and think about ways and means to give it added strength and stature.

There were several areas of the business which were of concern to him at that time. One was the turnover of men. It had been the practice to recruit men in the Spring; train them and lose them at the end of the season because, in those days, the business was forced into inactivity during the winter months.

Another problem was training. Martin was convinced that, if men were given the *scientific* background involved in tree care, as well as being taught the *practical* methods, they would develop a more professional attitude toward Tree Surgery.

It was also believed that the time had come to incorporate the business and establish a more formal type of organization. Further, it was felt this would provide the opportunity to attract outside investors because increased operating capital was greatly needed.

The solutions to these problems were vital steps in the building of a business which grew from a humble start, involving John Davey and three of his sons working in one little Ohio town, to when in 1959 it employed fifteen hundred people doing more than eleven million dollars worth of business with crews working in almost every state in the Union and Canada.

The ways these problems were solved are worthy of some detailed examination, because they were the foundation stones on which the Company was built. Also, those early decisions established a philosophy of a restless searching for constant improvement which became an important influence throughout the organization, serving it well in the years which followed.

VI   A Corporation Is Born

Martin L. Davey and his wife returned to Kent on December 1, 1908. It was on February 4, 1909, that the Company was incorporated and a new name was established, "The Davey Tree Expert Company." It was selected because it seemed to be descriptive of the enterprise.

The articles of incorporation stated that the corporation was formed for the purpose of the care, preservation, cultivation, propagation and sales of trees, shrubs and vines, and the practice of landscape architecture.

It was further stated, that the capital stock of the Company would be 50 thousand dollars divided into 500 shares of one hundred dollars each. In August of 1910 capitalization was increased to $75,000. The signers of the articles of incorporation were: John Davey, Martin L. Davey, Harmon L. Carson (who was married to Belle Davey, the only daughter of John Davey) Fred L. Allen and Charles W. Bishop, local Kent business men. John Davey was elected President of the new company and Martin L. Treasurer and General Manager.

The original stock was divided among Father John and his children, Belle, Martin and Jim. A block was set aside for Paul who was then in school. Another block was held as treasury stock for future financing. Father John immediately signed his shares over to his wife who was a prudent money manager.

Wellington was not a part of the new corporation and did not receive any of the original stock, although corporate records of 1910 show that he voted thirty shares and was elected a director.

Wellington, like youth in every generation, felt the urge to try his

Wellington Davey (left), Jim Davey (right)
doing an inspection of a cavity
filling made several years earlier.

own wings. With the encouragement of the family he operated tree surgery service in the Pittsburgh and Cleveland areas and later in Michigan.

In 1928 the Davey Tree Expert Company had some assignments in California, dealing with trees in the desert and in dry climatic areas. Since it was a highly technical assignment, it needed someone with a great depth of knowledge about trees. A proposal was made that Wellington take on this assignment, which he agreed to do.

As a result, he founded Davey Tree Surgery, Ltd. It grew to be a successful company due to the technical skill of Wellington and the management and organizing skills of his son, Keith L. Davey. The Davey Tree Expert Company acquired certain assets of the California company in 1969.

Wellington made valuable contributions to the science of Tree Surgery by playing an important role in developing sectional cavity filling, special saw cuts in pruning, and an engineered system of box-cabling, bracing, and soil drainage systems to carry off excess water in heavy soils. Some of these led to important patents.

Obviously, the success of the California Company came about long after the incorporation of the Davey Tree Expert Company. There were many victories and some disappointmets in between for Martin and his management. While they solved many problems, one that seemed to defy them, and particularly Martin, was finding outside investors for the Company. Shortly after incorporating in 1909, he spent a considerable amount of time trying to sell stock to leading business men in Kent. This effort did not meet with a great deal of success. After about eighteen months he sold $15,000 worth of stock to outsiders. Many who were approached felt that the business was a fad that would be short lived.

Many years later, in reviewing these frustrating efforts to attract outside investors, he stated, "My time would have been more profitably spent in trying to develop the Company's volume."

While stock sales were a disappointing effort, Martin was quick to understand the reluctance of investors to commit themselves to a new enterprise, in a new industry. He felt that those who did were entitled to every bit of the handsome profit they made on their investment when he bought them out a few years later.

Finding backers for a new business is always a difficult and arduous task. In order to solve this problem, many entrepreneurs give up more and more of their business to investors until, before they know it, they are on the outside looking in on something they thought was uniquely their own. Martin had a proposition of this nature laid before him. A group of men expressed their willingness to put up a substantial sum of money *if* they could have control of the business. He wisely refused the offer, fearing that the people who would most likely be hurt by such an arrangement were the members of his family and his original backers.

Trying to find investors and seeking other ways to finance the business took a great deal of Martin's time and energy.

Maintaining an adequate supply of working capital was a spectre that would haunt the Company for many years. Its very success helped to aggravate the problem. As the business grew, there was an increasing need for money to finance expansion and the Company was growing at a rapid rate. At the end of the first year's operation of the new corporation assets of $58,000 were reported at the annual meeting (held in January of 1910). One year later, in 1911 assets had leaped to $91,000.

Part of the financial pressure was due to the practice of not billing a job until it was completed. Since many of the assignments in those early days were involved with large estates, jobs would last for several months, which meant money had to be advanced for wages and materials, tying up substantial amounts of capital. It wasn't until years later that a system of partial billing was installed.

The members of the family tried to help by restricting their salaries and taking no cash dividends in order to build up a reserve. In 1912, when the money problem was particularly acute, Martin turned to the banks for help. Although the Company had a small line of credit, it was not enough. So, he approached the City Bank in Kent and arranged for a $5,000 loan. To get the money he had to agree to some rather stiff terms. The bank demanded that the Company pledge its accounts receivable at the ratio of two-to-one as security. They further demanded that, as accounts were paid off, the bank could select those which would replace them. Davey was also required to hire Harry H. Line, as financial adviser and pay him $50 per month during the life of the loan. His duties were to supervise the collection of accounts, and advise regarding disbursement of funds and generally on matters of finance and financial policy. All the while the battle for working capital was going on, other activities were being carried out to add vitality to what was then a budding enterprise.

VII   Organizing for Success

In 1910, Martin was re-elected Treasurer and General Manager of the Company. At the same time the Board of Directors clearly spelled out his duties and responsibilities. He was placed in charge of the business and was granted hire and fire authority over all employees, to fix compensation, to borrow money by pledging the assets of the Company, to enter into contracts on behalf of the Company and to do all things incident to the conduct and expansion of the Company's business . . . a nice neat all-encompassing statement that definitely established who was the Boss.

As Martin started to organize, he established the salesman as the key figure in the field operations.

He developed a table of organization by dividing the marketing area into territories. Each of these was assigned to a salesman responsible for profit and for all of the crews in his territory. A foreman was in charge of each crew. The sales assignment included getting enough business to keep the crews busy, and to schedule the work in a way that would avoid lost time resulting from long trips between jobs. The salesman and the foreman worked out an estimate for the cost of a job. Then it became the foreman's duty to see that the work was done within the price quoted. He was also responsible for keeping costs down but not at the sacrifice of the high quality Davey insisted on delivering to all of its clients.

To get the kind of performance Martin felt he had to have, he took great pains in the selection of manpower. And nowhere was he more careful than in choosing salesmen. He not only looked for men who were persuasive, but for those who had executive ability as well. No one got on that staff by having just a nice personality. Martin wanted to know the man's goals and why he wanted to sell Davey tree service. He also looked for men with more than a casual interest in trees. There were several in-depth interviews before Martin made a decision on hiring a salesman. After the selection was made, a substantial amount of time and money was invested to properly train the candidate. He had to know trees and their care and be able to discuss both intelligently. In fact, Davey salesmen became walking encyclopedias on trees. Some of those selected had a head start in tree knowledge because they had been promoted from the field crews. But no matter how strong their technical background was in tree care, their education never stopped; they were apprised of new developments through technical bulletins and, on occasion, brought back to headquarters for refresher courses and postgraduate study.

The care in choosing these men was a wise investment of time. They were recognized as an outstanding sales staff. Paid on commission, they enjoyed an excellent income. Several of them were able to earn more than the president of the Company. That never bothered Martin. He said, "When the salesmen make money the Company does too."

An equal amount of care was taken in the selection of foremen. These men were picked from the crews and knew every facet of tree care from having done, in actual practice, all of the things required to properly care for trees. They, too, needed an unusual combination of qualities. They had to be leaders to develop harmonious working relationships between the men and to motivate them to have pride in their work; they needed initiative to make on-the-spot decisions; they also needed tact and diplomacy to properly deal with clients while work was in progress. They were also expected to develop a close association with the tree owners. Their ability in this direction is best demonstrated by the number of lasting friendships that were built through just this kind of relationship. In addition to all of these activities, the foreman had to have physical courage as well, for when a job was considered too dangerous or too difficult for his men, he moved in and did it himself.

Crew members were also carefully screened. Martin looked for men of intelligence who might be promotable. Many of these men came from farms which seemed quite natural. Oddly enough, though, quite a few came from cities. There appeared to be a common denominator which attracted these men, whether they came from a rural or urban background, and that was an interest in trees, and the opportunity to work outdoors in a fascinating new industry. There were several basic qualifi-

Front Row: M. C. Clark, Amherst, Mass., James A. Davey, foreman, Kent, Martin L. Davey, business manager, Kent, F. A. Cutter, assistant foreman, Amherst.

Second Row: Ray C. Queen, Kent, W. H. Walker, Amherst, Mass., E. A. Adams, Ft. Dodge, Iowa.

Back Row: H. Eberle, New York, F. M. Hollis, Cleveland, W. C. Clancy, Oberlin, L. G. Vair, Ravenna, C. A. Thompson, Amherst, Mass., Two Unidentified, Ross A. Wiley, Bethesda, Ohio, C. A. Sampson, New York.

cations that were mandatory. Men selected had to be familiar with tools and know how to use them; they had to be physically strong enough to do the work; above all they had to be men of good habits; drinking was not tolerated and smoking on the job was not permitted. Every effort was made to make up crews with men of similar backgrounds. The reason it was necessary for them to get along with each other was because the men worked and lived together, which meant any forced idleness of crews during inclement weather could result in unpleasantness unless they had some kind of common interest.

There was a good reason for all the care taken in the selection of manpower. Men in the field played a vital role in the success of the Company. Never-the-less it was remarkable the kind of men who were attracted to the business. The work is hard. It can be dangerous. But it offers the right mixture of both physical and intellectual challenge that is attractive to an unusual type of men.

A good example of the kind of men drawn to the profession, was A. F. Baker, teacher, college man and Olympic Track Star, who joined the Company in 1907. In 1969, at the age of eighty, he put together a rather comprehensive record of his adventures as a Tree Surgeon.

He was eighteen years old when he went to work for Davey and had just finished teaching in a one room country school in Ohio. He had planned to enter Oberlin College in the Fall, and to earn money for expenses had considered working for a farmer for twenty dollars a month and his board. But before he took that job he learned that the Davey Tree Company was hiring men, paying them fifty cents an hour and were willing to train men to do the work. This seemed like untold riches, besides providing a real adventure in travel. He applied and was hired.

As Baker told it, he was born in Ohio and the largest city he had ever been in was nearby Springfield, Ohio. But now he was to go to New York and work along the beautiful Hudson Valley with the possibility that he might visit New York City itself.

In those days in order to get to the headquarters of the Company, located in Tarrytown, it required an overnight trip on a lake steamer from Cleveland to Buffalo and then a train ride through the beautiful Hudson Valley to Tarrytown . . . a rare adventure for a man of Baker's limited experience.

The work orders had an excitement of their own. He soon found himself assigned to estates owned by people whose names were legendary. He worked on Washington Irving's estate "Sunnyside," those of John D. and William Rockefeller, J. K. Lewis, General McAlpin, the estate owned by the Macy's (of department store fame) and others of equal stature. Many of the owners were interested in the work and discussed it with the Davey men, giving Baker and others, a knowledge that these men were down-to-earth people in spite of their fame and fortunes.

The Company was always on the lookout for promotable men so it was not strange that Baker moved ahead rapidly in the business. In the first summer he was promoted from "Tree Skinner" to Foreman. In the second year he was making estimates, and during his third year Martin offered him the position of Manager of a new office which was being opened in Chicago.

Since this would have meant leaving college he turned down the offer, ending his career with Davey in 1911. It was during this year he qualified for the 1912 U. S. Olympic Team.

The years he spent with Davey stayed with Baker all of his life. At the age of 81, he "doctored" a tree for his sister with a cavity filling and trimmed the top using the skills and the tools acquired over sixty years earlier.

Baker was one of many "Tree Surgeons" that made a mark on the Company. But his written recollection provides an important record of what "Tree Surgery" was like in its early formative years.

Some idea of the physical requirement can be gained from his remarks in this direction.

Bearing in mind that he was a trained athlete, he said, "Participating in college sports put me into pretty fair physical condition, but those first ten days or so of summer Tree Surgery made bed very welcome at night."

He went on to point out the reasons for this by saying, "Footholds in tree tops made trimming easy. But coming down the trunk with no footrest and two or three nubs to cut off, called for a rope around the tree and around the "Tree Surgeon's" waist. Then, with knees and hand, we held ourselves in position to cut off those last couple of nubs, which did something not only to develop muscles but lungs and heart as well."

The reason for this physical demand was that Davey Tree Surgeons have never been permitted to use climbing spurs, except on trees to be removed, because the holes left by spurs provide entry for tree damaging insects and diseases.

He further pointed out that ladders often were not long enough to reach the spot where work was to be done. Also, ladders were not always available because of the difficulty of getting equipment into remote locations.

In cases like that, it was not unusual for men to throw a rope over a strong limb and go up hand over hand. Baker reported on an incident like that which resulted in his only fall. He was working on a large Black Oak with thick scraggly branches starting about thirty feet from the ground. The nearest ladder was about a quarter of a mile away. Rather than go back for it, he decided to throw a rope over the lowest branch but failed in his efforts. Then he decided to shinny up the tree. At about twenty-five feet from the ground muscles rebelled and down he went. Fortunately he was not seriously hurt and was back on the job after a four day rest.

In spite of the danger of falling, Baker revealed that Davey men were very much at home in the trees, so much so that they would jump from one limb to another. While safety-minded executives of the Company would have had a fit of apoplexy had they known about the fool-hardy chances the men took, it never-the-less demonstrated the physical courage the men had. Baker also pointed out that to shinny eighty feet or more up a tree was not really an activity for the faint hearted.

It was clear from Baker's report, and from those of others who have spent their careers with Davey, that there was an exclusive bond of fellowship among these men. It stemmed from living together, sharing difficulties, success, and even danger. Somehow, unless one had shared in those experiences, he was politely made to feel like an outsider.

The carefully recruited army was getting into the field; however, there was much more to be done before the job of organization was completed to Martin's satisfaction.

VIII   The Davey Institute of Tree Surgery

M artin's care in the selection of manpower was remarkable on two counts. He was only 23 years old when he joined his father as a full partner so his business experience was limited. He had little opportunity for any kind of training in the selection of people, or for that matter, in any other management skills. There were no professional personnel consultants available. Even if there had been, it's doubtful that his struggling company could have afforded them. In the area of personnel selection he was at least 25 years ahead of his time.

There was another problem relating to manpower that had been nagging the Company. It was the turnover of crew members because of the seasonal nature of the work. The constant retraining of men was expensive; besides it prevented building a reservoir of manpower from which future foremen, supervisors and salesmen could be drawn.

The solution was found in 1909 when the Company founded the Davey Institute of Tree Surgery. Its purpose was to hold men by offering them a winter activity to foster their personal growth and provide scientific knowledge to supplement their technical skills, which would make them much more valuable to the Company and to its clients. It also added another dimension to their work and made their jobs much more meaningful and interesting.

It took some doing to get the men to accept the idea. For, after all, not everyone who entered the business shared the enthusiasm or had the vision of the founders. Martin finally offered to raise the pay a dollar a day, for anyone who enrolled in the school, effective at the start of the next season. Twenty men accepted the initial offer and made up the first class which was scheduled to last for three months.

*Early Davey school in Kent's Hall
over the Kent National Bank.*

After the Institute had become firmly established, it was patterned
like a college and the course of study was expanded to three, four-month
terms, given during three consecutive winters, starting in early December
and ending in early March. The faculty was made up of prominent educators recruited from leading colleges and universities. The curriculum
included subjects like Botany, Entomology, Plant Pathology, disease and
insect control, soils, fertilization, and the theory and practice of tree surgery. Students were also taught Accounting, Business English and Business Ethics.

To further foster a college atmosphere there was an extensive athletic
program which resulted in some outstanding teams. All students took
part in a physical education program to keep them in top shape. While
all of this provided an outlet to soak up the energy of a group of healthy
young men, it also built an esprit de corps which was an important asset
to the Company.

It wasn't long before the competition to attend the school became
keen among the younger and more ambitious men. In contrast to Martin's
initial effort to recruit students, later classes were made up of men care

fully selected and *invited* by the Company to attend. Students were brought to Kent by the Company and paid enough to cover their living expenses during the school term.

Obviously, the Institute was an expensive operation because it followed the Davey adage of, "Do it right or not at all." But it paid off in many ways. It minimized the scramble of hiring and training at the start of every season.

Experienced men were on the job, ready to move into the field as soon as the weather permitted. The school also brought into existence a group of trained professionals, ready to take on greater responsibilities when they were offered. The experience and education of the men was also a very powerful sales tool. Most of all, the type of work, and the kind of men who were doing it were very pleasing to the clients.

Another step the Company took at this time to keep the crews readily available was to develop winter business in the South.

In order to accomplish this, Martin selected several of the best salesmen and sent them South to secure business. At the same time he offered crew men the opportunity to join them. A great many accepted . . . . glad to get winter work.

This effort met with some modest success as revealed in Company records of 1910 which reported crews working on the La Gonda Planta-

Perry Hudson and squad on Long Island in 1919.

tion in Patterson, Louisiana. Others were working in places like the State House Grounds in Columbia, South Carolina. Jim Davey was reported working in northern Alabama.

In spite of all of this activity it took several years before southern operations were profitable for the Company. It did, however, accomplish the basic objective of having experienced crews ready to move into the field as soon as the big season in the North began.

It has been bold creative ventures like the Davey Institute of Tree Surgery and the Southern expansion that have helped to keep the Davey Tree Expert Company far ahead of any one who tried to compete with them in the industry which they founded. The school, and everything it stood for and produced, is an example of the courage and foresight of Martin and his management team, who were willing to spend and invest during the slack seasons when the operation was not profitable. Less venturesome men would have chosen a different course.

But Martin had little time to sit back and philosophize. There were other areas calling for equally vigorous solutions.

IX   Loyalty Rewarded

The success of the Davey Tree Expert Company was largely brought about by the dynamism of Martin. But he, and the men who followed him, recognized that the loyalty and industry of the men and women who worked for the Company also played a major role in bringing about that success.

In recognition of that contribution the Company has always had special concern for its employees. Many benefit programs were instituted. None of them sprang from the roots of paternalism but were based on a sincere respect and high regard for people *as individuals* and a desire to help them reach basic goals.

Through the Company, Martin was able to help employees reach their personal objectives because one of his great strengths was his understanding of what people were seeking from their work. Nowhere is this insight better expressed than in the opening paragraph of an editorial he wrote for The Davey Bulletin, titled "The Sound of Success" in which he said in part, "Every normal man wants to succeed. He wants success not only for the financial benefits involved but for the personal satisfaction that goes with it. It is this enlightened self-interest that is the great moving force in the world of practical affairs."

In the beginning Martin had to persuade men that Tree Surgery provided a great deal more than temporary work. He had to convince them that this new science was laying the foundation for a whole new industry that would provide financial rewards and a very satisfying career. He not only talked and persuaded but backed up his words with action which resulted in programs to help men achieve their basic desires.

The company-sponsored school was one of the programs which serves as a vivid demonstration of the kind of action the Company was willing to take to help men attain greater personal growth. Employees working for competitors and lacking this training, were little more than laborers, doing what they were told without knowing why, or what effect their work would have. In contrast, Davey men were professionals and knew precisely what they were doing—and why. The men who finished the course of study never lacked for job offers from competitors. The few who succumbed to these offers, soon found their skill exploited by their new employers who never seemed to show any reluctance in advertising the fact that they had "Davey-trained men" on their payroll. This competitive action helped to further convince those who chose to cast their lot with Davey, that they were indeed superior to all others who worked with trees.

Martin was always a great believer in acknowledging merit. In commenting on this he said, "When you quit recognizing human merit you never get it any more." As a result of this conviction, salary increases were given before they were asked for. A system was established whereby salaried employees were reviewed every six months. Field men were reviewed monthly. If raises were merited they were granted.

Men who demonstrated that they had the ability to take on increased responsibility were promoted. Over the years the "Davey Bulletin" carried numerous reports of "tree-skinners" who were doing the work in trees being moved up to foremen in charge of crews. Others were promoted from the Field Crews to supervisory or executive positions.

He acknowledged the contribution made by several of his key men and women by naming them to his Board of Directors. In explaining this action he said, "If these people are valuable in making day-to-day decisions, then their thoughts and opinions are equally valuable in formulating policy for the Company."

However, before they were elected to the Board they were asked to buy stock in the Company. Martin explained this action by saying, "I want to be surrounded by successful people not just cogs in a machine. We want them to realize they are part of the Company, are capable and aspiring, and who think of the future."

In 1928 others were offered a Class "B" non-voting stock in the Company, but on a very selective basis. To be permitted to buy shares in the Company was considered a privilege and even though it was offered no one was obliged to buy it.

The offer was made to salesmen and foremen who were considered key men in the organization. The stock was offered to them at about two-thirds of its computed worth. Cash sales were given a five percent discount. However, a time payment plan was offered which enabled buyers to pay for their purchases over a ten year period at six percent interest. The Company guaranteed that the interest rate paid would never exceed the dividend rate of the Company. In the event of permanent injury or death, the man or his estate would be given a paid-up stock certificate.

There was also a limit on the amount of stock an individual could buy. It was set at $10,000 for salesmen; and $5,000 for foremen with ten years service or more. Not everyone was permitted to buy these maximums; the amount was determined by a point system. In the case of a salesman he could score thirty points for length of service, thirty for quality, and forty points for sales volume. If a salesman scored seventy points on this scale he was permitted to buy $7,000 worth of stock. Criteria for determining the amount the foreman could buy was based on length of service and quality of workmanship produced by his crews. Any complaints received about the performance of a foreman's crew became the criterion used to measure the quality factor. Work was not only scrutinized by clients but was evaluated by the salesmen and screened by the Chief Experts (who were in a supervisory position established by the Company to keep close tabs on field operations).

The stock purchase plan offered to key men was also designed to make these highly trained specialists feel aware that they were an important part of the total operation and the success of the Company depended on their actions in the field.

In addition to the privilege of buying stock, foremen who were with the Company four years were given a thousand dollar twenty year endowment insurance policy. At the end of seven years of service, the policy was increased to two thousand; at ten years, to three thousand.

The Company paid all of the premiums on the policies. The only restrictions were that the men were not allowed to borrow on the insurance or surrender it for cash without the consent of the Company.

The whole purpose of the stock purchase plan and the insurance program was to help the men build a comfortable estate for themselves. However, the stock purchase plan had to be discontinued during the depression of the thirties.

During that low economic period, Davey shares, like all other stocks, shrunk in value. Further, the Company was forced, by prevailing conditions, to discontinue paying dividends. All of this upset participants in the stock purchase plan. Many of these people apparently never realized that any investment can go down—as well as up. In any event, the Company recognized that, instead of helping, the plan was hurting employee relations. So it had to be discontinued.

The amounts of money mentioned in these programs seem rather small when judged by today's standards. But all this was going on in a period from 1910 to 1928, a time when a man could buy a comfortable home for his family for two or three thousand dollars.

While Martin did a great deal to help his people gain financial security he also demonstrated that he had high regard for their opinions as well. If a new policy was to be initiated he would discuss it with the people involved before it was put into effect. He explained his reasons to them and accepted constructive suggestions. While at times this slowed the decision-making process, in the end it saved time and tempers. It provided another benefit as well. When people felt they were a part of formulating a course of action, they supported it with enthusiasm instead of having the sometimes reluctant acquiescence imposed policies tend to create.

It was back in 1909 that Martin conceived the idea of an annual convention which brought the salesmen and the foremen to Kent. The meetings were scheduled to take place early in March, coinciding with the end of the school term for the Davey Institute of Tree Surgery.

During this convention period salesmen and foremen held meetings to discuss field problems. And, out of their combined experience, they would try to find answers to them. After several days of separate sessions both groups were brought together to report what had gone on, and the solutions agreed to.

This proved to be a productive effort. It not only helped bring about solutions to field problems, but it also promoted a more closely knit organization. It resulted too, in informing the home office of what was going on in the field.

Probably the highlight of those conventions occured in March of 1926. It was planned to celebrate the twenty-fifth anniversary of the publication of John Davey's book "The Tree Doctor."

To mark the occasion, Will Rogers, humorist, actor, writer, and current affairs commentator, was brought in as the headliner for the celebration banquet. Business leaders were invited in addition to the Company personnel. It was a glorious occasion with about 2,000 people attending the banquet, including Davey employees from office, shop, warehouse, students, convention people and others.

Further, balcony seats at the Akron Armory were distributed by re

DAVEY TREE EXPERT CO. OFFICE FORCE, ABOUT 1925

Left to right: (*girls*)
Pauline Deibler
Fanny Allen Renouf (J. Norvil)
Gladys Englehart Cherry (Robert)
Marjorie Sampsell
Irene Sawyer George (Allen)
Iva Johnson Bottorff
Myrna Young Smith (Barton)
Ruth Lyons
Bernice Hill
Sarah McCoy Deubner (Ted)
Lucille Warth
Eleanor Young Cole
Marion Shremp Nellis (Joseph)
Opal Bennett
Martha Bechtle Palmer
Margaret Goodman (Paul)

Frances Austin Hynton
?
Louise Bayless Mooren
Hazel Carey (Ed)
Marie O'Bierne Girtner
Virginia Stevens
Elsie Judson
Alice Marria Fleshman
Pearl Chamberlain
Ida Fahrny
Bessie Hawk Jones (Harold)
Molly Landis (Tom)
Constallota Deltorio
Marjorie Barton Shorts (Milo)
Mary Holland O'Bierne
Gertrude Perk (sister of present
    mayor of Cleveland)

Peg Boyle Cook
Alice McCoy
Mildred Cook Myers
Mae North
Helen Connors
Margaret Geisinger
Ruth Luff Myers (Franklin
    "Whitey")
Back Row, left to right (*men*)
Charles "Pat" Fadely
George White
Orrin B. Crosser
Stuart Stevenson
Elmer Sill
Harry L. Swain, Sr.
Hugo E. Birkner

SALES CONVENTION OF DAVEY TREE EXPERT CO., KENT, OHIO, JANUARY 31, 1939

1 Paul H. Davey, 7-4-11
2 U. L. Throm, 5-1-15
3 E. P. Metcalfe, 10-7-10
4 W. R. Williams, 7-26-15
5 Martin L. Davey
6 W. E. Bailey, 3-26-09
7 H. I. Spellacy, 7-28-15
8 D. Q. Grove, 5-27-10
9 C. L. May, 4-1-16
10 B. L. Brittain, 7-11-16
11 A. S. Anderson, 3-13-16
12 Hugo E. Birkner, 9-5-16
13 O. B. Crosser, 9-2-19
14 P. E. Hudson, 5-11-09
15 C. V. Bistis, 4-1-12

17 C. O. Brittain, 4-19-21
18 D. B. Magruder, 9-19-21
19 T. J. Adams, 6-24-19
20 M. W. Staples, 5-4-15
21 H. P. Granger, 5-30-24
22 E. L. Lambert, 5-4-20
23 A. J. Landberg, 9-24-23
24 S. D. Maud, 6-1-22
25 G. H. Bone, 6-18-26
26 G. W. Landis, 5-24-20
27 H. O. Lehman, 2-9-25
28 H. C. Wilson, 8-6-24
29 D. H. Fowler, 6-27-23
30 A. M. Swanson, 9-17-21
31 V. A. Hill, 10-22-26

33 F. F. Lofgren, 3-26-25
34 F. W. Strufe, 7-15-27
35 Ray Gustin, Jr., 3-19-22
36 F. E. L. Killen, 6-14-26
37 W. H. Knowles, 5-13-25
38 J. F. Allen, 6-27-27
39 W. C. Lauck, 6-5-25
40 J. M. McNees, 6-23-26
41 G. B. Chenoweth, 8-13-27
42 J. L. Heston, 6-27-21
43 Benton Larson, 3-29-29
44 L. F. Irvine, 6-1-25
45 H. E. Cooke, 7-11-27
46 W. H. Parker, 9-15-30
47 H. J. Rice, 7-9-23

49 D. F. Hayman, 3-31-28
50 C. J. Keller, 3-25-29
51 E. I. Kabel, 8-24-36
52 R. H. Sands, 6-12-33
53 T. L. Swanger, 4-5-34
54 H. E. Johnson, 6-22-36
55 J. C. Turner, 6-7-29
56 J. W. Brittain, 4-10-36
57 O. E. Hildebrand, 4-4-30
58 R. A. Hemingson, 3-25-35
59 Harry J. Miller, 3-30-36
60 E. S. Pirtle, 4-25-34
61 C. G. Wood, 5-14-35
62 C. J. Mahady, 10-3-38
63 R. R. Lewis, 5-13-26

quests to relatives of employees and townspeople in the area, to give them the opportunity to hear Will Rogers, who was at the height of his career. Every seat was filled with S.R.O.

Then, during the 1934 Convention, one of the actions taken by Martin became a legend, to be told and re-told through the years. During the depression of the thirties, the salesmen had piled up substantial debits and were unable to pay back what they owed. This resulted from the fact that even though commissions were based on sales, regular weekly checks were sent to the salesmen to enable them to live. Often sales were so low, commissions did not cover the money advanced which resulted in ever-increasing debit balances. Martin, with his keen insight into human nature, knew there could be nothing more discouraging than a load like that on a salesman's back. On the second day of the convention, when gloom and doom seemed to be ruling the day, Martin exploded the news that as of that very moment he was wiping the slate clean. The accumulated salesman's debts, amounting to $100,000 were wiped off the books. The announcement put the salesmen into a state of shock. It took them nearly twenty-four hours before they could respond to this generous act. When they re-acted, it was with renewed enthusiasm and resolve to do an even better job for their company.

Martin was thoughtful of the people in the Company in many ways. He treated them with dignity and as personal friends. He seemed to have a knack for remembering how important little things are to people. For instance, he initiated a tradition in the Company which goes on to this very day. On a person's birthday the president of the Company sends a personal letter of greeting. Another is sent to husband or wife, if the person is unmarried, it's sent to the employee's mother. Also, children of employees, between the ages of six and eighteen, receive a "Birthday Letter" from the president, if they are living with their parents.

Martin showed his respect for field employees in other ways as well. He would not stand for supervisors brow-beating them, insisting people should be led and not driven. On extremely rare occasions clients were abusive to the crews. This was not tolerated and there were standing orders not to accept further business from people who evidently lacked self-control.

While he did a great deal to make careers with his company rewarding in every sense, he was no "patsy," blind to the failings of a few. He had no patience with those who were long on talk and short on performance. Neither would he tolerate laziness or dishonesty.

In spite of careful screening of people there were bound to be some

57

on the payroll who were found to have undesirable characteristics. Fortunately they were few in number. But when they were discovered, corrective action was taken immediately. One incident illustrates this point. A foreman with a great many years' experience became demanding and refused to follow orders. He wired the company if they did not do things HIS way he would resign. He was badly needed at the time as he was on a very important job, but when his ultimatum arrived Martin promptly fired back this response: "Good bye—good luck—God bless you. Period"

While Martin had a high regard for the forces in the field, he expected them to reciprocate by providing outstanding performance in their assignments.

It was John Davey who pointed out why this was so important by saying, "Those who buy our service are entitled to their money's worth."

He always felt a deep obligation to those who turned to him during the early days of Tree Surgery, and later to the Company for service. Consequently, he felt the Company had a responsibility to provide service of the highest quality. Father John urged those who had charge of hiring to, "Seek people who want to give clients a dollar's worth of work for every dollar spent."

This desire of the Company to provide quality performance has been carefully nurtured and kept alive throughout its existence.

Toward this end the following set of rules establishing lines of authority and accountability, which were agreed to during the 1910 convention, appeared on the front page of the "Davey Bulletin" week-after-week starting with the July 9th issue of that same year.

RULES OF THE COMPANY

The following rules were framed during Convention Week and will constitute the platform of the Davey Tree Expert Company. All differences will be adjusted according to it.

In order that no one may ever have the excuse, "I didn't know about any such rule," this platform or set of rules will be published every week in The Bulletin. These rules were not made for effect but will be rigidly enforced whenever violations come to the knowledge of the responsible parties.

PROMPTNESS.
Foremen and men must be at work on time.

TOOLS.
A full set of tools must be possessed at all times by each foreman and workman.

SMOKING.
Smoking is absolutely prohibited during working hours. Examples will be made of all violators of this rule.

DRINKING.

The use of intoxicating liquor of any kind is prohibited. Its use will be cause for dismissal without warning.

CONDUCT.

Be gentlemen at all times. Boisterous conduct or profane language will not be tolerated.

BOOKKEEPING.

Strictly adhere to all rules for bookkeeping set forth by the Company. They are made for your convenience as well as the Company's.

PERSONAL APPEARANCE.

Men are required to present a personal appearance which shall maintain the dignity of the profession.

FOREMEN.

All foremen are considered as working foremen. The less time taken to properly supervise the work, the better.

RELATIONS BETWEEN MEN, FOREMEN, REPRESENTATIVES AND COMPANY.

(a) The men are at all times responsible to their foreman. The foreman is vested with power to suspend a man who in his judgment is detrimental to the Company's interests. Upon conference with the representative of his district, the man may be discharged if the case merits dismissal.

(b) The foremen are at all times and in every way responsible to the representative. The Company will require the utmost degree of cooperation between them in every instance.

(c) The representatives are responsible to the Company for all conduct and business in their respective territories.

Then, some twenty years later, a "Standardized Methods and Don'ts" was written by David Quincy Grove, Chief Expert, which set forth the one right way to perform every single operation associated with Tree Surgery. It also listed forbidden practices.

In addition to the standardized practices Martin also included forty-nine "Don'ts For Tree Surgery." These might well have been entitled, "How to Provide Thoroughly Professional Service." Each one of the points emphasized common sense ways of providing the kind of performance clients appreciate.

While Martin was exacting in enforcing high standards of conduct and workmanship, he had a reputation of being open and fair. As a result, there was an intense loyalty built up between him and his employees. At no time was this better demonstrated than during the depression of the early thirties, when there wasn't enough cash to meet the full payroll. When this happened, Martin wrote letters to each of the men and explained the condition and the reasons for it. He did not try to "sugar coat" the issue, but gave them all of the facts as he knew them. He explained that he could make partial payments and asked them to tell him the minimum amount of money they needed to get along. The response was terrific. Even in the worst of times, some men said they would take nothing till the condition righted itself. At other times, there were those who offered their personal savings to help tide the Company over a rough spot. Some of the men took only enough to keep their families fed and clothed. Everyone tightened his belt. Fortunately those conditions were of short duration and all of the people received every penny coming to them.

It was a rare relationship that existed between Martin and the people who made up the Company. In spite of all of the work and investment and sacrifice that was poured into this association by both sides, two words seem to describe it all—*mutual respect.*

X Why Politics?

It's almost unbelievable that while Martin was providing strong leadership to the Company, laying the ground work for growth by establishing a philosophy that would extend far into the future, he was also starting what became a distinguished political career.

He was elected Mayor of Kent in the fall of 1913. He was re-elected for a second and third term in succession. He was elected to the United States Congress, in the fall of 1918, as representative from the 14th Ohio District, to serve an unexpired term and the following full term as well; at the end of that term, he was out of Congress for two years and then back again for three successive terms. He was elected Governor in 1934 and served two terms.

Many have asked, "Why politics?" After all, Martin had only been with the Company seven years when he was elected the boy Mayor of Kent at the age of 29. While there was every indication that the Company was on the road to success, there were many basic problems that needed attention. It appeared to questioners, that the building of the business would provide all of the challenge anyone would want, or need, to build a satisfying career.

His father, for whom he had a great deal of respect and affection, opposed his entering politics, as did some of the key people in the Company. There came a time when he, too, had some questions about his pursuit of a political career. He wondered if the same effort expended in seeking public office, might not have been more effectively used to further develop the business.

In answer to the questions raised, including his own, he offered two principal reasons for seeking public office by stating, "In politics one works exclusively with people, and an elected official has an opportunity of doing a little bit better job in serving them."

At the same time he said, "Many people think of the Tree Business as exciting and different from all others, which is true. But the managers of the business miss many of the interesting and challenging problems and find themselves confronted with the same burdens as those of any other enterprise—money, sales, and policy. But in politics there is a certain amount of drama. Besides, it offered me an outlet for my excess energy."

The last statement offers a clue as to why he was moved to pursue a dual career. He was blessed, or cursed, with an inner drive which was possessed of a voracious appetite, demanding to be fed more and still more in the way of personal accomplishment. From his earliest years he had committed himself to "Show the world." He never gave up trying to do just that.

It is also easy to understand how he might have felt the necessity for another activity because of the outstanding progress the Company was making. There was a firm acceptance of Tree Surgery as a valuable service. Letters of appreciation and approval were frequent and from knowledgeable people, like Dean Fernon of Toronto University, Department of Forestry, who wrote a letter enthusiastically expressing his high opinion of the Davey organization and its work.

By 1911 the Company was operating in thirty-one states and in Canada. The business had grown to the point where the home offices had to be expanded to take over the entire second floor of the Allen Building in Kent, Ohio.

As early as 1910 the Company showed signs of maturing. In January of that year the Board of Directors established a Finance Committee made up of Harry H. Line, Fred L. Allen (two local successful business men) and Martin. The Committee met weekly to formulate plans to expand the business and to counsel with the General Manager and Treasurer of the Company . . . both of these offices held by Martin.

It was at that time, also, that some of Father John's philosophy was put into action. He was of the firm belief that, "It is thought which moves the world." In making this statement, he was emphasizing the fact that ideas are a valuable commodity and no organization could have too many. He also feared complacency and stated, "We are good, but not good enough." He urged that every effort be made to discover new methods and refine established ones, so the treatment of trees might be improved.

That there were those in the company who shared his views is attested to by the fact that two Cornell University Professors, Rankin and Illingworth were retained to teach in the Davey Institute of Tree Surgery and to conduct research under fellowship grants financed by the Company. Results of their investigations were to be presented to students of the school and were also to become the property of the Davey Tree Expert Company. Rankin's principal areas of investigations were a study of fungous diseases and heart rot. Illingworth was primarily interested in developing ways to rejuvenate old apple orchards. He also was active in developing spraying techniques.

It was during 1911 that Martin conceived the idea that if he could get business on the grounds of the United States Capitol and the White House at Washington it would provide prestige, which would be useful in promoting Davey services.

Toward this end he sought the assistance of Judge David Ladd Rockwell and several other members of the City Bank, who had purchased stock in the Davey Company. He asked for their help in arranging an introduction to the proper people in Washington. It was Martin's hope this would get him a hearing with the men who could make a proper decision.

Judge Rockwell arranged a meeting to enlist the aid of John O'Dwyer, leader of the Democratic party in Toledo. He agreed to help and set up a meeting with Congressman James M. Cox, later Governor of Ohio. He in turn arranged an introduction for Martin to Elliott Woods, Superintendent of the Capitol grounds.

Woods turned out to be a serious and business-like gentleman who toured the grounds with Martin and listened to his presentation, promising that he would consider it. But weeks passed and no order came through.

Martin decided that more drastic measures were called for. He returned to Washington and toured the grounds on his own. During this inspection he found some of the maple trees covered with insects. He clipped off one of the branches and carried it to Wood's office, where he laid it on his desk. Woods was shocked and immediately arranged for another tour of the grounds with Martin. This tour was much more thorough and serious than the first one. And *this time* an order for tree care came through rather quickly.

It was during this assignment that the Davey Tree Expert Company was called upon to treat the famous Washington elm which was in very poor condition. Legend has it that George Washington stood under this tree while supervising the building of the original Capitol. All of this led

63

Martin L. Davey and Elliott Woods, Supt. of Capital Grounds examine Washington Elm on Capital grounds in Washington, D.C., an example of long life through proper surgery.

to further work on the White House grounds, as well as all other government institutions and for prominent people in the city.

About this same period the Canadian Government engaged the Davey Company to save the trees on their Parliament Grounds in Ottawa, Ontario.

Over the years, skills of the Davey Tree Expert Company have been called upon to preserve thousands of other historic trees. However, many of these calls were from groups who were unable to pay for tree work. In fact, there were so many of these requests for free service the Company could not handle all of them. There was just no way it could have afforded to honor all of them. However, they did accept a limited number of these assignments.

One of the most interesting, as far as Martin was concerned, dealt with a great horse chestnut tree at Fredericksburg, Virginia. This was one of thirteen trees, planted by George Washington, in honor of his mother Mary Ball Washington, and to commemorate the thirteen original states. The trees had been planted between her home and that of her daughter and son-in-law, Colonel and Mrs. Fielding Lewis.

Only one of the trees remained at the time—a magnificent specimen, tall and stately, with a reasonable amount of vitality. However, its trunk and main branches were hollow from internal decay. All of this had to be cleaned out, the cavity disinfected and properly prepared before receiving a Davey-type concrete filling to promote natural healing. It was also badly in need of extensive mechanical bracing and proper feeding.

All of this work was done at Davey Company expense. Several years later, Martin went back and was amazed and pleased at the way the tree had responded to treatment. He reported his thoughts as he viewed this beautiful specimen of a tree, planted by the hands of George Washington. He said, "This, and other leafy giants of its time, are probably the only things now living which were alive when Washington traveled this way. The great trees are the only links between the life of his time and ours. There is something grandly historic about them, and there is a majesty in their stalwart forms."

In 1910, and the years immediately following, the Davey Tree Expert Company became a thriving enterprise. It was growing, expanding and reasonably profitable. But there were clouds of trouble appearing on

Successful surgery at the Capitol.

Davey men at work on a Tulip Poplar planted by George Washington in January 1785.

65

the horizon. Some of the problems were caused by the very success the Company was experiencing.

There were a number of men who witnessed what was happening with Davey and felt sure they too, could become a success in this new industry. Some were just handy men who would do most anything where a dollar could be gained. They hurt the Company because, in many cases, they lacked skill and knowledge to properly carry on the practice of "Tree Surgery," they "butchered-up" many of their tree assignments. In fact,

Tree butchery by amateurs.

this type of operator became known in the profession as "tree butchers." Photographic evidence of their work proves they properly deserved the name. Their "quackery" created disillusioned clients for tree care and tended to give the industry as a whole a bad image.

Others who entered into competition, were men who had been trained by Davey at a great expenditure of time and money. Among them were several salesmen who decided to pull out of the Company in 1913. They said their action was to protest Martin's participation in politics. Whether this was the reason or not, became a moot point. The fact remains they left the organization, and for awhile it hurt the Davey Company. These salesmen were key men who had been placed in positions of great trust by Davey. They knew the clients and the potential of their territories. Because of this they were able to attract some business for themselves.

The Company called on Jim Davey to correct the situation. And he did. He went into one territory after another and, by dint of hard work, determination and dedication to the cause, he outsold each of the deserting salesmen in turn. As fast as he got one territory in shape, another good and loyal salesman was put in charge, then Jim moved to the next one. In a surprisingly short time he turned the situation around.

As a result of this defection by a few of their trusted employees, the Company was forced to engage in some very expensive litigation. These men deliberately and seriously infringed on patents owned by Davey.

Again, Jim was called upon and did an outstanding job of securing necessary proof and supporting evidence, to help the Company win its cases.

Little of tangible value was collected from these suits. Most of the people had few if any assets from which damages could be collected. Later, it caused Martin to observe rather ruefully that, "A patent only gives you the right to sue."

The high cost of this litigation reflected itself in a poor profit year in 1914. However, while this early competition upset the management of the Company, they finally had to accept it as one of the penalties of leadership that went along with starting a new industry. It was decided to ignore the competition as much as possible but warn the public about the "quacks" in the business; and to concentrate every effort to improve the service being offered by the Davey Tree Expert Company.

Many people who plunged into the business based on the Davey Company's success failed to realize that they were seeing only the tip of the iceberg and that there was a great deal below the surface that was not quickly visible.

There was much more to the success of Davey than technical knowledge. In fact, its accomplishments were the result of a precisely balanced set of skills covering a broad spectrum of talents. It required skilled management, research, promotion, training people, the courage to explore unplowed ground, and, most of all, a dedication to high ethical standards so aptly expressed in the Davey battle cry, "Do it right or not at all."

XI Promotion, A Key
to Success

The value of advertising was one of the elements most often overlooked by those who plunged into the tree business hoping to duplicate the Davey Company's success.

Yet, according to a statement made by Martin, advertising was one of the key factors in the development and growth of the Davey Tree Expert Company. He said, "In spite of the tremendous value of the service that we render the public in saving trees and in the improvements that we made in the training and techniques of our men, our business could not have reached sizeable proportions without the powerful and constructive influence of advertising. Without it, our business would have been a relatively local and unknown one. It was our advertising that unlocked the doors in tens of thousands of American homes for our sales representatives. Naturally, we had to deliver fine service and make good in the eyes of our clients after they gave us the orders. But it was advertising that made it possible for our salesmen to get the majority of their interviews and receive favorable consideration from tree owners."

The first Davey ad appeared in 1910 in the fall issue of "American Forester." Martin who had prepared the ad admitted later that it was a rather crude affair. But it worked and produced a number of inquiries which resulted in orders, some of these from as far south as Richmond, Virginia. This was fortunate, because it came at a time when the Company was trying to build a winter business in the south. The Richmond orders kept the crews busy while the salesmen were developing business in the deep South.

Shortly after the appearance of that first ad, the Company arranged for the firm of J. Horace MacFarland of Harrisburg, Pennsylvania to take over the advertising. Two pieces of sales promotion done by this firm seemed to stand out in Martin's mind. One was entitled, "Our Loving Friends The Trees." He doubted the use of the word "Loving" stating that, "It was overdoing a good thing by making it appear that trees were capable of love."

A later booklet, "New Life in Old Trees" written by MacFarland, was remembered for its excellence and because it was successfully used in direct mail advertising.

In 1917, the J. Walter Thompson agency of Chicago was selected to handle the advertising. They were chosen because they had a Cleveland office which made it much more convenient for the Davey organization than the location of the previous association.

Thompson had the Davey advertising account until the Depression, when business conditions forced the Company to temporarily discontinue its advertising. The program was resumed in 1937. At that time, the assignment was given to Meldrum & Fewsmith, a Cleveland based advertising agency.

One of the early highlights of the Davey advertising was the appearance of its first four color advertisements which appeared in 1910 in magazines of national circulation.

Advertising was used to solve one of the concerns of the Company which was that the bulk of the business seemed to be coming from large estates. This of course was good business, and in itself helped to produce other orders. Many of these estates were featured in the Company's advertising and other promotional material. But it was feared that it left the impression that "Tree Surgery" was something that only the wealthy could afford. Besides, there was a strong feeling within the Company that there were a great number of others who could use the service to advantage—like the farmer with an orchard or the home owner with one or two trees that added their protective shade and beauty to his property.

The advantage of the smaller jobs was that they were done quickly and paid for in a short time, which improved the cash flow. In addition, very often these jobs could be used to fill-in between larger assignments, which helped to keep the crews more steadily occupied.

But to reach this market was *not* a short term effort. In fact it went on for many years. As late as 1927 the Company advertised that it did a total volume of $2,400,000 serving 17,417 clients and that 7,390 tree owners paid less than $100 for the care of their trees.

Broadly speaking the advertising effort was low key and not given to wild claims. It was generally built around the aura of romance John Davey had built up that trees were friends of man. The messages also explained what could be causing a tree's decline and invited readers to have their trees examined by a Davey Tree Doctor. They promised that a true report would be submitted. If they were healthy, or in need of care, owners would be so informed.

Davey men lived up to the promise made in their advertising to provide an impartial diagnosis. If trees required care, the owners were told what was needed to be done and how much it would cost. On the other hand, if trees did not need care, owners were so informed and told how to keep their trees healthy. If the Davey inspection revealed that a tree was too far gone to respond to treatment, the job was refused. Certain trees were on a "black list" because it was known that they would not respond to treatment. Likewise, work on trees such as the Chestnut (which was subject to blight) was turned down.

Often Davey men would be asked to go ahead in spite of their careful analysis. Sometimes owners would say, "It's my money, so go ahead." The reply would be, "But it's our reputation."

Innovation was one of the keys to the success of the Company. It was no different in its advertising. The Davey Company was one of the early users of radio network time as a sales tool. In 1929 Martin contracted for the "Davey Hour" to be broadcast from New York City every Sunday afternoon over a network of twenty-four stations stretching from Boston to Kansas City. The program consisted of old time popular music, none of the selections being less than ten years old. He was advised not to use this type of music. Both his advertising agency and officials of the network strongly suggested that he should use Symphonic programs or the contemporary music of the time, which was Jazz.

Martin ignored this advice, based on his personal observations of large singing groups who always seemed to choose—and enjoy—the old time favorites.

He also remembered a great ovation given Madame Ernestine Schumann-Heink, the great operatic star when she sang "Home Sweet Home" at the close of a program of strictly classical music. He said the same thing happened when John McCormack, the famous tenor, ended a similar program by singing "Mother Machree." He reasoned that by using older, more popular tunes, he could tap people's memories and associate the Company with pleasant past experiences, enjoyed by the listeners.

During the hour long programs Martin would devote 10 to 15 minutes to discussions of some phases of tree care. He would often warn people about the "quacks" in the business. There were no tapes in those days so it required a weekly trip by train to New York for Martin to make his Sunday afternoon presentations leaving Saturday night and returning Sunday after the broadcast. The response was tremendous and proved to be another factor in making the public tree conscious while producing business for the Company. The program was so successful that it was continued for nine months in the fall, winter and spring of 1930 and 1931. The final series appeared through April of 1932. Then the depression hit with the devastating force of an avalanche—and the world was never the same again.

One of the interesting sidelights of the radio program was the interest Harvey Firestone Jr. expressed in them. He was very favorably impressed with the format of the Davey program and admired Martin's weekly tree presentations—so much so that he persuaded Martin to write speeches for him to use on a program his own company was about to put on the air. Martin agreed and the Firestone people were well pleased with the talks, which were used for a period of 3 months.

While people in the Company were quite lavish in their praise of advertising and the effect it had in helping them build a successful business, there were other promotional efforts that made important contributions in the same direction. The excitement and glamour of broadcast and publication advertising often made it easy to overlook other programs. The truth of the matter is, that the Davey Company almost from its very beginning carried on a "total communications" program that was a very sophisticated one.

The Davey Bulletin falls into this category. Born in 1910, and still published, it has served the Company's interest in many ways. As the operations of the Company spread, it was feared field people would feel cut-off from the home office. The Bulletin did, and is doing, a good job of eliminating this feeling of isolation. It publishes the things that the Company does, but also informs them about their associates—where they are working—what they are doing—who is getting married—who passed away and who has had a baby. It tells the kinds of jobs being done, explains and tells about new techniques. During his life-time it also provided Martin with a vehicle to reach people and inspire them through his editorials.

The Davey Tree Expert Company over the years has published an almost endless number of booklets that contain valuable information on

The John Davey elm being dug on farm 3 miles west of Kent.
The tree measured 50 ft. tall and was 15 inches in diameter.

The John Davey elm being planted at Roosevelt
High School in Kent on March 5, 1930.

73

the care, use and preservation of trees. These are valuable texts that help teach people that trees can and should have a long life, if given the proper care.

Another important communications activity was the use of publicity. As the interest in tree care grew, so did the fame of John Davey, known throughout the world as "The Father of Tree Surgery." A great deal of the publicity was built around him. He provided an ideal subject for he was a living, breathing "Horatio Alger" hero. Here was the poor immigrant who came from a humble beginning and rose to fame and fortune. It was the American dream—come to life.

That Father John was good copy was demonstrated by a tribute paid him by Elbert Hubbard, the famous essayist, entitled "A Brother To The Trees."

In 1909, Hubbard engaged the Davey Tree Expert Company to do some tree work on his property. In the course of the assignment, he and John Davey developed a lasting friendship. As a result of observing the men working on his trees and getting to know the humble man who started it all, he wrote one of his famous essays, part of which is produced here, because it is indicative not only of Hubbard's feeling but those of many others as well.

The book, THE TREE DOCTOR, encased in lead, being installed in the John Davey elm.

THE TREE DOCTOR, and its lead casing, after recovery from the John Davey elm when it was removed due to Dutch Elm Disease in January 1971.

Martin L. Davey, Jr., and Alexander M. Smith examining THE TREE DOCTOR after its 40 year stay in the John Davey elm.

"It is a great man who can introduce us to the divinities that surround us, and make us realize our sacred relationship. I met such a man some months ago. His life work so appealed to me that I grew suspicious of myself and refused to write of him until I knew him better. That is to say, the very excess of my regard made me go slow.

"A year has passed since I first heard of this man of power whom I would discover to all Roycroftia and the lands that lie beyond. 'How there was a man sent from God, and his name is John'—John Davey. He is sixty years old, but looks forty, and at times acts twenty. In figure he is slight and slender, but in strength he is like the silken cord that held the god Thor—it stretched but never broke.

"John Davey is the Tree-Man, or the Tree-Doctor, or the Father of Tree-Surgery. I like to call him the Tree's Brother. No man I ever saw so mixed with the elements—no man I ever knew so blended with the leaves —no man I ever knew possessed such a sympathy for waving, swaying saplings as this man.

"His life is all so bound up in trees and the birds that live in their branches, that he would forget his own needs if someone did not look after him with the same loving care that he bestows on trees. Fortunately John Davey has a very practical wife and they have four sons and a daughter, all tree folk, who realize that it is not quite time to adopt the Elijah habit of life, and bank on the ravens.

"John Davey is a genius, for a genius is one who has the faculty of abandonment to an idea, or a cause. He is without a taint of degeneration—a genius with the innocence of childhood, and the intellect of a man. John Davey does not know he is a Pantheist, but that is what he is.

"The actions of men have two effects—primary and secondary. Often the secondary effect is of more importance than that of the primary. John Davey calls himself a Tree Surgeon. His treatment of decayed trees is parallel to the work of a dentist on a decayed tooth. He arrests decay and works for health. This is Davey's primary work. The secondary result of his work is not its effect upon the tree or the owner of the tree, but the influence of his work on society. This to me, is the vital issue.

"In carrying forward this work of looking after sick trees, Davey is assisted by several hundred young men, whom he has selected and trained for the business. When you hear of a 'Davey gang' being at work somewhere, go and see them. They are a type. Bare of head and arm, brown, small or of medium size, silent, they work with a precision, an intelligence and an earnestness that is a delight to see.

"John Davey's heart is his art. And his art is the art preservative.

Davey is a result of the constructive desire of the times. He is a product —an answer to prayer, sent to fill a demand.

"A few years ago, and the life of such a man would have been a tragedy, dark and dank as can be woven of the warp and woof of time. We know what had happened to the simple, direct, frank and honest men in the past. Imagine what would have happened a hundred years ago in New England if a man had preached the divine spirit of God manifesting itself in the trees."

Others wrote about John Davey in a less poetic way. It all helped to win acceptance for Tree Surgery and to further the cause of the Company.

There are two stories that are told and while they deal with advertising they provide some insight into the Company as well.

John Davey was always his own man. This was demonstrated when at one time Martin had an outdoor advertising campaign ready for release. It was illustrated with a photograph of John Davey who always wore a neatly trimmed beard, which gave him a professorial appearance. But on this particular day he walked into the office sans beard. He had decided that beards were unsightly and unsanitary and had his immediately shaved off. But Martin was flabbergasted and, to put it mildly, more than a little upset. What could or should be done about all of the expensive posters? After the initial shock was over it was decided to go ahead with the campaign because no one would recognize John Davey's face without the beard.

Another incident demonstrates the utter faith Martin had in advertising, but also indicates that the Company had a tough Board of Directors. The facts are gleaned from the minutes of a Board meeting held in May of 1921. During this session, Martin had asked for approval to spend an additional $25,000 for newspaper advertising. The Board must have been dubious about this request as indicated by the kind of agreement that was made. This was a very substantial sum, especially at a time when the whole economy was severely depressed. The Directors granted approval of the expenditure with the provision that if the volume of business for June, July, August and September did not reach $350,000 Martin would be required to pay $10,000 of the $25,000 out of his own pocket. A man had to have faith in what he was doing to agree to that kind of deal. While this said a lot about Martin it also demonstrated that the Board was not about to risk the Company's money on just any kind of proposition.

Later, in another meeting during that same month, the Directors relented a little by agreeing that if the net profit for the year reached $75,000 Martin would be paid a $10,000 bonus. Even in this action the Directors proved they were not about to spend, unless they got a return for the money.

All of this is not to say that the Board was afraid to spend money, particularly on advertising. Year after year minutes from its meetings indicated it approved increased expenditures for this part of the business. In fact, the provisional approval on the newspaper advertising was an isolated incident.

While it has been indicated that Martin had complete faith in advertising and promotion as a way to build business, he also felt that there was a fringe benefit. He said, "The advertising had a positive effect on the officers of the Company. Claims made in the advertising increased their desire to continue to live up to the claims. It also had a good effect on the employees. It gave them pride in their work, their profession and the Company."

The promotional activities are interesting in themselves, but they again emphasize that the success of the Davey Tree Expert Company consisted of many building blocks bound together with a mortar, which was a mix of courage to venture into uncharted territory, and a dedication to "Do it right or not at all."

XII Victory and Sadness

The period from 1911 to 1923 was to witness a period of fast moving change and progress for the Davey Tree Expert Company. It was designed to be a time of victory. It was also to be a time of sadness.

One of the first of the changes to take place was in May of 1912, when Harmon L. Carson, husband of Belle Davey, and director, was elected Secretary of the Company succeeding Leonard G. Vair who had resigned. Carson held the post until 1960 when he retired.

The following year, 1913, the Board created a new position . . . assistant General Manager. Chester C. Dumond was elected to fill it. He had studied Forestry in college and had been one of the original crew to work in the Hudson Valley. He had been a Foreman for several years and was one of those who had been picked to head a crew during the Company's early efforts to build business in the South.

It was in August of that same year that the Directors discussed the advisability of establishing a correspondence course to teach Tree Surgery. The course was to be patterned after the curriculum used in the Davey Institute. In October they set a budget of two thousand dollars for this project. Minutes from subsequent Board meetings reveal that promotion of this course was aggressively pursued through 1916, when a budget of $8,500 was established to advertise the correspondence school.

The basic reason for initiating the correspondence school was to provide knowledge and training for field men who for some reason could not attend the Davey Institute of Tree Surgery. It also was a valuable aid to hiring. Obviously men who were interested in studying the material, were logical candidates for employment.

The correspondence school is another indication of foresighted management and its ability to prepare for the future. It is all the more remarkable, in light of the fact, that 1914 was not a profitable year for the Company. There were two events which were responsible for that situation. The first of these was the heavy legal expense caused by patent-infringement cases. The other was due to World War I which was getting under way in Europe, creating uncertainty in the minds of people, causing them to be very cautious in their spending.

In face of these conditions, the Company had put into operation some very conservative fiscal policies. As a result, they were ready for prosperous times that were just ahead.

By 1915, the enormous purchases being made by France and England, stimulated the American economy. Davey, along with other companies, felt the effects of this, not only in increased volume, but the prices of everything, including wages started to escalate.

Soon, Davey management found themselves in a squeeze between rising costs and an attempt to sell their services at a pre-war price. They realized the necessity of raising prices but this was something they had always hesitated to do in the past. In fact, Martin had proposed a modest increase in prices years before, and had been over-ruled by the Board Members, who chose instead to keep their salaries and dividends low. However, this time, no other solution presented itself. So it was agreed to adjust the price schedule.

True to his philosophy of discussing important changes with the people directly involved, Martin arranged to have all of the salesmen brought into Kent, where the proposal to raise prices was laid before them. At first the men were reluctant to endorse the price change, sure that it could not be sold. After some rather lengthy discussions they were persuaded to try. Soon, after returning to their territories, they found the new price schedule could be sold without difficulty.

By 1916, business was booming. The Company was able to buy out some of the early investors, paying them a handsome profit. It was also at that time that a policy for $60,000 was placed on Martin's life, naming the Company as beneficiary. Martin urged this action as a way to establish a borrowing source, and because it would be an asset that would grow in value each year.

A number of years later in reviewing some of the mile stones of the

Company, Martin said, "That period was the beginning of real prosperity for our enterprise. It was a time when we were able to expand all of our programs much more quickly than ever before."

The war in Europe was still raging. There was increased discussion about America entering the war on the side of the Allies. Finally, it happened, on April 6, 1917, the United States declared war.

The immediate effect was to further accelerate business. The Davey Tree Expert Company again found it necessary to raise wages and prices. Orders for Tree Surgery were easy to get. The big problem was to supply enough men to do the work. Profits were the best in the Company's history.

But again in Martin's words, "There was a terrible price to pay for all of this prosperity. It wasn't long before casualty lists began to appear in the daily papers, serving as a grim reminder that it was now 'our war.'"

All too soon, the war had a direct effect on the Davey Tree Expert Company and on the Davey Family.

There was plenty of business for the Company, but the Draft was taking men into the army at a rapid rate. The Davey field men were prime targets. Most of them were unmarried, all of them were intelligent and accustomed to a rugged outdoor life, which put them in excellent physical condition. They were exactly the type of men the armed forces wanted. Further, there was no basis on which the Company could ask for a deferment for these men.

In 1917, it was possible to find and train replacements. But by the next year, men were leaving for the armed forces at such a rapid rate, there was little opportunity to replace them. This condition became even more difficult, when many of the experienced foremen were drawn into service. The result was that by Armistice Day, the work force was down to eighteen salesmen and seventeen field men.

The men who left Davey to enter the armed services were not forgotten. The Company kept in touch with them with frequent letters, many of which were written by Martin. The Davey Bulletin was also sent to them, which made it possible for them to keep abreast of what was going on in "their" company.

In spite of a sadly depleted work force, the Company was in a good financial position, due to management's ability to husband its resources. As soon as the war was over, most of the experienced men rejoined Davey. General business conditions continued on a high plane in 1919, and the Tree Business started to operate at a rapidly increasing rate.

Plans were made to develop the future growth of the business by building an even firmer foundation under it.

The plans included an expansion of the scientific resident school, a more ambitious research and experimental department, improved field training procedures for new men, and the creation of field supervisors, to be known as "Chief Experts." These men were charged with the responsibility of developing uniform field operating procedures. Along with all of this, a more elaborate advertising program was planned. To accomplish this, the Board approved a $40,000 advertising budget . . . the largest in the Company's history up to that point.

Two important personnel changes occurred in 1919. Jim Davey was named manager of the New York office and the Board elected Hugo E. Birkner Assistant General Manager.

All the while these plans and actions were going forward, the Davey family was experiencing anxiety over the youngest brother, Paul. He had enlisted in the 116th Engineers of the United States Army in May of 1918, shortly before his marriage to Maxine Beckwith, of Oberlin. The family had received a letter from him in October, informing them that he was moving up to the front. Weeks, then months, passed with no word. Nothing . . . just a dreadful silence. Finally, he was located in France, recovering from a serious case of pneumonia. Shortly after his discharge in February of 1919, he rejoined the Davey Tree Expert Company as head of the Field Forces and the Research Department.

For the first two years after Paul's return, the Company was still enjoying prosperity. But, in the second year, 1920, economic storm signals started to appear. Some of the basic business indices like steel production, electric power output, and car loadings were declining, giving warning that there were economic problems ahead. Unfortunately, the signs were all too true. By 1921 the country was in a severe depression. Government bonds had dropped to eighty, and many people suffered severe losses in the stock market. Davey was able to maintain a reasonably good volume during this period, but profits left something to be desired. The depression lasted through 1922. But, by 1923, the economy snapped back and continued to move upward.

As the economy corrected itself, sadness was to strike the Davey family again. On November 9, 1923, John Davey, the inventor of the science of Tree Surgery, died very suddenly of a heart attack, at the age of 77. His passing was mourned by the great, and near great, and far beyond the city of Kent, where so many of his early struggles took place. He was followed in death by his wife, Bertha, who passed away the following year, on December 10, 1924.

Their passing marked the end of an era, which recalled Dickens' famous words, "It was the best of times, it was the worst of times."

While John and Bertha Davey enjoyed a full and satisfying life, they were denied the opportunity to witness the growth and accomplishments of their youngest son, Paul.

XIII   New Directions

Paul was a remarkable person in many ways. He was talented in several directions, yet kind, understanding and blessed with a good sense of humor. It was quite clear that Martin thought Paul was someone special, although he was mildly critical of him in one area. He remarked, "There were times when I felt that Paul was too sympathetic with the men and let them get away with things I would not have permitted."

Among his many talents was Paul's athletic ability. During high school and college he developed into a baseball pitcher of more than ordinary ability. He was good enough to get an invitation from the Cleveland Indians, to try out for their team. But he turned them down, and the opportunity for a major league baseball career, because he had an offer to sell books in Indiana and he wanted that experience.

Paul, like all of his brothers and sister had been exposed to the tree business all of his life. His direct experience was gained by working for the Company during summer vacations and for a fifteen month period between high school and college.

When he rejoined the Company after the war, field operations were carried on much as they always had been. The work was done by skilled men using simple hand tools. Each man owned a set of tools which included a selection of chisels, a mallet, a slick, a point gauge and tree saw. The Company tool box had in it a bull saw, brace, a set of bits, a hack saw, ropes and a grinder to keep tools sharp. There was also a materials box filled with things like coatings for covering tree wounds, fertilizer, nails and nuts used on bracing rods.

While the tools used to do the work were quite simple, transporta-

*Paul H. Davey
in January 1960.*

tion to the job was equally so. Men and materials were often hauled to the job by a local teamster, and it was not unusual to use public transportation which was cheaper and often faster.

Paul Hershey, who joined the Company in 1926, and rose to President in 1964, recalled using street cars to get to a job. Tool boxes were loaded on the back platform, but the long rods used for bracing presented another problem. To solve it, several men would get window seats, hang their arms outside and hold the rods on the side of the car until they got to where they were going.

Not only were the rods big and cumbersome, it took a bit of doing to get them made. It was up to each foreman to find a local machine shop, which would cut them to size and thread the ends.

In light of these circumstances, as head of the field force and research department, Paul Davey had set two main objectives for himself; mechanize the operations and build a bigger winter volume of business. Although the Company had developed business in the South, i was far from satisfactory. There was still the problem of losing trained men because of the winter layoff. The school kept some men occupied during the winter, but even this was not enough to keep a full force on board in the off season. Hiring and training new men each spring was an expensive operation.

It was in 1921 that a series of events took place, which had a far reaching effect on the Company and helped to direct its future course.

It all started when Wesley Hollister, who had been a professor in the Davey Institute, was elected Mayor of Kent, for 1921-22. He appointed Paul Davey to the post of Commissioner of Shade Trees. While in that position, he was approached by the Northern Ohio Power and Light Company for permission to clear some trees so they could run power lines through Kent.

Paul was concerned, because, as he put it, "I thought they wanted to trim the trees at the base." In other words, cut them down. To add to his dilemma, he recognized the importance of electric power to the community. There was, also, a public relations aspect to be considered. Property owners always took a dim view of having their trees "butchered" by unskilled workmen from a utility company. Paul knew that if that happened, he and Hollister would be in for some rough abuse from Kent residents. It was, also, a delicate situation for executives of the Power Company. They didn't relish the idea of creating a mass of irate customers.

As a way out of the situation, Paul proposed that the Power Company let the Davey Tree Expert Company do the work. The Company readily agreed. The result was a two-fold benefit for the utility. Property owners were pleased because the work was done in a professional manner, which protected the health and beauty of their trees. This, of course, added lustre to the image of the Power Company. Davey did the job for far less money than the utility company had planned to spend on the project, a pleasant experience for any management.

While the project worked out to the complete satisfaction of Northern Ohio Power and Light, Paul was not earning a great deal of applause from his own Company. He had taken this assignment over the objections of both Father John and Martin. They took a rather dim view of the rough way utilities generally handled trees. However, Paul was quick to recognize a potential in this type of business, that both his father and brother apparently failed to see at the time.

The success of the Kent project, led to other similar assignments. It wasn't long before Paul's judgment was to be justified. As a result of that first satisfactory experience, other job assignments of a similar nature were given to the Company. Milford W. Staples, dubbed "Biff" by his co-workers, was one of the early line clearing specialists. He recalled doing work for utilities around Kent, Ravenna and Medina. He also recalled another job for Bell Telephone, which required clearing lines, starting in Toledo and running fifty miles south.

Meantime, Paul kept pushing the Sales Department to go after utility business. Soon, a big order came in from Boston Edison. This started the real growth of serving utility companies.

The development of this type of business was one of the most significant events in the growth and success of the Davey Tree Expert Company. It ranks in importance, along side of the book "The Tree Doctor," and Martin's early success in the Hudson Valley. Some idea of its growth and importance to the Company, can be gained from figures which show that in 1960, it amounted to $7,053,000 out of a total volume of $11,834,000. It did provide the added advantage of keeping more men employed on a year round basis. Lines both in the North and South had to be cleared, and kept clear, twelve months of the year. Its real importance was to be demonstrated during the great depression of the thirties and in World War II. On both of these occasions, it was the one source of business which kept the Company alive and healthy.

All the while business from the utilities continued to grow, Paul was far from idle. Almost from the day he rejoined the Company, he started to seek ways in which some of the procedures could be mechanized. About 1920 he started to explore the various types of power spraying equipment available on the market.

Up to that time the Company had done very little in the way of large volume spraying, primarily because it was a hard job, demanding huge amounts of muscle power. However, the Company possessed a great deal of knowledge about insects and diseases which attacked trees and other plants. John Davey, from the very earliest days of Tree Surgery, was familiar with these enemies and how to combat them with available chemicals. Later, the research carried on by men like Hollister and Illingworth, added tremendously to previously acquired knowledge of the subject.

The efforts to combat insects and fungous diseases were somewhat restricted by the few spray chemicals available at the time. "Biff" Staples pointed out that the materials were limited to refined oil for scale; lime and sulphur, used as a fungicide; arsenate of lead, for destroying insects and Bordeaux mixture, also a fungicide. Incidentally

Bordeaux mixture was not originally designed to be used as a fungicide but was put on grapes by French farmers to discourage people from stealing and eating their crops.

In spite of the limitations, a great deal was done with the available chemicals to combat insects and diseases. The challenge was to find an efficient way to spray large areas and to reach the tops of large trees.

Toward that end, a power rig was put together in 1921. "Jerry" Landis, who spent his entire career with Davey, reported on his experience with that early power spraying outfit. He said, "The first power sprayer of any size, was bought in the Spring of 1921. Its brand name was 'Friend,' and it had a spray output of twenty gallons per minute. It had a 300 gallon tank mounted on the front end of an Akron Thomart, a one ton truck, which was assembled in Kent, Ohio."

Landis went on to say, "The rig had been driven to Greenwich, Connecticut by Ray Landis (Jerry's brother) accompanied by Wesley Hollister. They did a few spray jobs in the area. The rig was then turned over to a man by the name of Charles E. "Pat" Fadely, picked to be the Foreman. I was the truck driver and mechanic. Our first job was in Boston, where we sprayed for the Gypsy Moth. The first year we did $5,000 worth of spraying in five weeks. We drove the truck from Boston, Massachusetts, to Philadelphia, Pennsylvania, and did spraying there and in Connecticut, New York, Long Island, and New Jersey."

From that early experience, spraying developed into an important and lucrative service offered by Davey. It grew from $5,000 reported that first year, to a volume of $481,000 in 1960, which was about four percent of the total business for the year.

Another service which Paul Davey helped to develop and actively promoted, was the moving of large, full grown trees, which began in 1926. In the beginning the work was done with some rather crude equipment. It consisted of a solid tired White Truck with a power winch mounted on it, and a two wheeled cart. The use of this equipment, made it possible to move trees up to nine inches in diameter.

Later, working with outside sources, Paul Davey helped to develop a more sophisticated piece of equipment. It consisted of a trailer with two wheels forward and six in the rear to support the ball. After the root ball had been carefully dug and properly prepared, the trailer would be backed up to the excavation and arms would be extended up and along side of the trunk, where they would be securely fastened. Then the tree would be winched down on the trailer bed. This piece

1928 tree surgery truck.

Early air compressor.

Early spray equipment at work.

Tree moving in the late 1920s.

of equipment made it possible to load from the rear or from the side of the trailer. Over the years this equipment went through a whole series of developments which finally included the use of hydraulic-powered booms.

Tree moving was a spectacular operation. For that reason it drew a great deal of favorable attention to the Davey Tree Expert Company. There were reports of trees being moved that weighed up to twenty-two tons.

Large tree moving was a specialized service. Men engaged in this part of tree care, had to know how to use the large, heavy and expensive equipment to get the most out of it. In addition the men had to know how to properly trim a tree that was to be moved and to correctly prepare the root ball. Also, there were certain trees which could not be successfully transplanted. In the early days of tree moving, most of the full grown trees which were to be transplanted were secured in rural locations and were known as "collected trees." Because of the special skill and knowledge required, not every crew was able to offer this service. In fact, before a salesman accepted an order involving moving a full grown tree, he had to get approval from the head of the department.

Paul Hershey related a story about tree moving which illustrates some of the difficulty encountered in that activity. Paul was a foreman at the time and according to him, an architect who was building a very fine home, wanted a large tree planted in front of it. When Hershey went to inspect the location, he found a deep, wide ditch between the road and the building site. Even worse, the spot the architect had picked for the tree's location, was on top of a steep knoll. It looked like an impossible situation. Hershey registered his concern with the architect, only to be told, "Mister that's your problem. That's where I want the tree." And that's exactly where it was put.

In order to get the equipment, and the tree on the property, Davey men built a bridge across the ditch. Then by an ingenious use of winches they got the tree up the steep grade. In commenting on this incident, Hershey was moved to remark, "It's a lot easier to spot the location of a tree with a pencil on a piece of paper, than actually doing it with heavy equipment."

There was a great deal of tree moving done to help eliminate the cold, stark appearance of new buildings. A good example of this, was the large number of trees which were planted by Davey crews, around the Treasury Building in Washington, D. C., as well as around many public and private buildings, in all parts of the United States and Canada.

One of the most spectacular tree moving operations, took place in Toledo, Ohio, in October of 1930. The public Library was being enlarged, but a magnificent Copper Beech tree, thirty-six inches in diameter, standing about sixty feet high, with a spread of forty feet, was growing on the site which had been selected for the new building expansion.

Davey people were called in to determine whether the tree should be cut down, or moved to another location behind the library. Ike Crawford, a Davey foreman and master tree mover, and Herbert J. Rice, the Toledo sales representative, and a skilled tree surgeon, agreed that the tree could be moved. However, the final decision was put in the hands of Biff Staples, who was the regional supervisor. He agreed with the two men that even though the tree was the largest that the Company had ever been called upon to move, the job could be done.

To move the tree a large power shovel was employed to dig a deep trench around it. Then a crew of coal miners was called in to undermine the root ball. As the men dug, they inserted ten by twelve inch timbers every foot or two. The timbers were blocked up at both ends, and pressed tightly against the root ball with driven wedges. Then a power shovel dug a deep, wide trench from the tree to its new location. Tracks were laid on the bottom of the trench and the tree was winched to its new location. It was estimated that the root ball weighed 107 tons.

Tree moving was an important service offered by Davey for many years. As time progressed it became of less importance, particularly as far as large, collected trees were concerned. The popularity of one story homes and commercial buildings eliminated the need for three story trees. Then as the super highways came into existence, it became more difficult to transport the huge trees which had been done with such a spectacular flourish in the past. However, tree moving is still carried on today and is one of the important services offered by the Davey Tree Expert Company. But the trees are no longer collected from rural locations; instead they are carefully grown on the Davey Tree Farm, located just outside of Wooster, Ohio. Trees of up to twelve inches in caliper are moved from the farm to many wide-spread locations.

In 1926, when Paul Davey was aggressively promoting tree moving service he was also actively continuing his search for ways to further mechanize Tree Surgery procedures. In the process, he developed an air actuated power tool for use in cleaning out the decay in tree cavities. The tool did the job it was designed to do. But, it fell into disuse in a relatively short time. This was partially due to the difficulty of getting

Franklin "Whitey" Myers on the job with a compressor
operated cavity machine in 1931.

a power source into remote work sites. This somewhat limited its use
and besides the tool was quite expensive.

By now it was becoming apparent that Paul was something of
a mechanical genius. The revelation was further demonstrated by still
another series of related inventions.

The initial success of power spraying encouraged Paul to seek out
larger equipment. There were big capacity air compressors available
but they were heavy, cast iron, water cooled, behemoths. He started to
look for an air cooled compressor. He was told there was none on the
market and that there had never been a satisfactory one produced.

This led Paul to the development of the first air-cooled compressor.
Everyone else who had tried to produce a piece of equipment of this
kind built it with the traditional metal used to produce compressors . . .
cast iron. Paul used a finned, aluminum head, which conducted heat
away from the engine, eliminating water cooling. The result was a compressor which was dramatically smaller and lighter than the giants that

94

were on the market and still it was able to match them in power output. It offered several other advantages as well; lower maintenance, easier cold weather starting, and lower fuel consumption. Between 1926 and 1929 the air-cooled compressors were built for the exclusive use of the Davey Tree Expert Company.

In 1929 Paul and his two brothers, Martin and Jim, founded the Davey Compressor Company. Events were to soon prove that this was the worst possible time to start a new business because it was the beginning of the Great Depression. In spite of an inauspicious beginning, the Company become a successful one, in both domestic and international markets.

Other inventions by Paul included the Davey Power Take-Off, which made it possible to use the truck engine to power auxiliary Davey equipment. An indication of his creative ability is the fact that he was granted fifty patents for his numerous inventions.

Paul Davey continued his direct association with the Davey Tree Expert Company for fifty years. He was a director of the Company until 1961 when he was succeeded by his son Paul H. Davey Jr.—who was at this time President of the Davey Compressor Company.

Paul's remarkable achievements gave the Davey Tree Expert Company additional strength to resist and survive the chilling winds which were to blow across the nation's economy in the depressed Thirties.

XIV   The Roaring Twenties

After the recession of 1921, the balance of the decade became known as the "Roaring Twenties," and offered a favorable economic climate for business growth so good, that many people thought those days would never end.

Even in that kind of atmosphere, business success called for a bold, enterprising management to maximize the available opportunities. This was particularly true in the case of the Davey Tree Company. It is so easy to record the success of new services like power spraying, line clearing and tree moving and forget what it took to make them a viable part of the business.

These broadened services meant management was faced with new experiences and demands. They had to establish warehouses and invest in rolling stock and special equipment. In the late Twenties they even found themselves engaged in the manufacture of air compressors. The days of operating with a few simple hand tools were fast disappearing. All of this demanded a fresh approach to the business, calling for greater capital investment and larger amounts of money to finance the operation of the business.

While management was finding answers to new problems, there still existed the perennial ones of competition, money and manpower that cried out for attention.

Occasionally, what appeared at first to be a serious problem turned out better than expected and offered a large measure of satisfaction, as a bonus.

One of these was an experience in 1921, which when concluded, filled the whole Davey organization with pride. At that particular time Elliott Woods, Architect of the Capitol, had appointed a committee to investigate the merits and demerits of the work and materials used in cavity filling by the Davey Tree Expert Company and one of its leading competitors.

The competitor used a wood product for cavity filling. The investigation revealed that this material cracked and disintegrated, sometimes within a year. In several cases, where bolting was used with this product, areas around the bolt heads caused serious damage to the tree, which the investigators blamed on salt used in the filler.

Examination of cavity work done by Davey, using a cement filling, and the patented method of applying it proved that it held up even on trees that had been treated several years earlier. It also demonstrated that the Davey method did indeed promote the healing process.

There still existed the problem of companies and individuals infringing on Davey patents. In 1922 there were thirty-five injunctions issued by United States District Courts, against operators who were guilty of infringing on the Cavity Filling Patent.

Finding the solutions to problems like these were victories of a sort, but to a degree, they were repetitious of earlier battles. They were like the delicious roast that is bound to lose some of its appeal the second time it is served.

The real excitement for Davey management was in the new services that provided growth at a very rapid rate.

Discovering new services was not the result of happenstance. They were the result of a restless searching for methods which would improve the practice and science of Tree Surgery. The thoroughness of Davey Research is amply demonstrated by the studies made on tree fertilization.

Paul Davey, as head of Research and Development, assigned Homer L. Jacobs to carry out studies on shade tree fertilization. Jacobs, known as "Red," joined the Company in 1922 and had a long and illustrious career with the Davey Tree Expert Company. It included teaching in the Davey Institute, Field Supervisor, Head of Technical Services, Technical Director, Vice-President and a Director of the Company. After his retirement he served as consultant to The Holden Arboretum, near Cleveland.

"Red" was soon to discover that there was little in the way of published material to help guide him in his new assignment. He found a great deal of material relating to forest trees and some on orchard trees. There was nothing on shade trees. It was known that John Davey got spectacular results in restoring trees to health by improving soil conditions. His methods for doing this were described in his book "The Tree Doctor." That was about the extent of the published information on shade trees.

At the time Jacobs started his research, the recommended method of shade tree fertilization stemmed from orchard practice which said to fertilize trees only in the Spring. This custom was the result of the conviction held by horticulturists of that time, that fertilization done during Mid-Summer and early Fall, would promote new terminal and cambium growth. The theory held that this new growth would be prone to Winter injury because it would not have time to harden before the weather turned cold. They also believed that any nitrogenous material, applied when the tree was going into a dormant state, would leach out before the tree had a chance to use it the following Spring.

In order to test the validity of this theory, Jacobs set up a study of 378 trees which included: Norway Maples, American Elm and Apple trees (which were often used as shade trees). The trees were divided into three equal groups, both by number and species. One group was fertilized in October of 1926, then was treated again exactly one year later. Another group was fertilized in April, 1927, and again in April, 1928. The same amount and type of fertilizer was applied to both groups. The third group received no fertilizer and served as a check group.

Results were carefully recorded from 12,000 measurements which included trunk diameters and terminal twig growth.

They discovered that the fertilized trees did dramatically better than non-fertilized trees, which might have been expected. The studies blasted the old theories because there was little difference between the growth and vigor of trees fertilized in the Spring and those fertilized in the Fall.

From a commercial aspect this resulted in a change of Davey field practice. Previously, fertilization of shade trees stopped after August first. As a result of this research the field force was instructed to fertilize until the end of the Northern season.

In the first year this extension of the fertilizing season resulted in the additional sale of $37,000 worth of Davey Tree Food. The fertilizer was a formula developed through Davey research. This material consisted of organic material for long lasting qualities, and chemical food elements for fast results.

This of course represents only one study. There were others. Even this one did not stop after two years. It continued and expanded to cover different species including Conifers.

There is another interesting aspect to Davey research. Bearing in mind that the Davey Tree Expert Company was not a corporate giant, and that it did not receive grants from a benevolent government, it was very generous in circulating its discoveries. Obviously patentable ideas were protected. But other valuable information was put into bulletins and widely circulated to agricultural colleges, experiment stations and other sectors of the scientific community which had an interest in improving shade tree care. For instance the research on shade tree fertilization was published in a bulletin and distributed to 2,500 interested people.

Many other studies were conducted. Among them were those concerned with the controls of insects; fungous diseases; and the response of certain trees to various conditions of climate, atmosphere, and soil.

In 1946 the Research Department of the Davey Tree Expert Company published a 211 page book called, "The Arboriculturist." It included previously published materials from 1935. It amounted to an encyclopedia of shade tree care. "Red" Jacobs was the editor.

The fact that Davey shared these studies with others, reveals that tree care was more than just a way to make money. The Company was dedicated to saving trees, if not by its own efforts, then by anyone who had a sincere interest in doing so.

The new ideas stemming from these research activities had a beneficial effect on sales volume. The year 1924 was a good example of what was happening and was to become an important milestone in Davey history. The Company had been straining for several years to put together a million dollar sales year. It appeared for a time that they would do it in 1923 but they fell short of the goal with a volume of about $810,-000. The following year sales reached $1,200,000. For any company the first million dollar year has a special satisfaction and significance. It was no less so with Davey.

Advertisements carried the message that this volume was done by serving 6,852 clients with 5,565 of them paying less than $200 for the service. In comparison 4,558 clients were served in 1923. While the Company was serving large clients, the management never seemed to overlook the value and the importance of the small client.

But in spite of whatever success they were having, Davey management never seemed to sit back with a sigh of contentment and say, "We've arrived." There was always a healthy feeling of discontent which underlined management's total commitment to "Do it right or not at all."

A good example of this attitude happened during the 1924 sales convention. Paul pointed out to the field men that 449 complaints had been received. That figure represented about 6% of all clients. The fact they satisfied 94% of the clients was not good enough. The goal was zero defects. Complaints were analyzed and men were told how to avoid them in the future. How easy it would have been to say, "We're batting .940, so that makes us better than good." The reply might have been in John Davey's words, uttered many years before, "We're good, but not good enough."

While management worked hard on its own to solve problems, like cutting down complaints, Martin was wise enough to use his salesmen and foremen to find solutions to problems. This technique was used to good advantage during the 1925 convention. Foremen registered strong dissatisfaction with the hit and miss way they were compensated for business they secured by their own efforts. They wanted a uniform plan, that was fair to all.

For a variety of reasons, foremen were a good source of business. But payment for this extra effort was at the discretion of the salesman in charge of the territory. As a result, some foremen were paid nothing, others received varying amounts.

The salesmen favored leaving the situation unchanged. They feared that if the foremen were encouraged too much, they might interfere with the salesmen's planned activities for the area.

In the course of the discussion, the atmosphere became somewhat tense.

Two of the foremen, who had success in getting orders, presented plans. One had a "two and five plan." It called for a payment of two percent from former clients and five percent on new business created entirely by the foreman's efforts. In addition he proposed a yearly cash prize for the foreman who secured the most business. The other was a "three and five" plan with a one percent bonus on each thousand dollars signed up.

After some spirited debate, Martin stated that the Company wanted a uniform plan, applicable to all territories. He proposed two percent for old business and five percent for new business, payable on settlement of the invoice.

As a result of these differences, the group decided to submit the problem to a board of arbitration consisting of three salesmen, three foremen and three people from management, one of these to be Martin. The result was a flat four percent commission paid to the foreman regardless of the source, one percent to be paid by management and three percent to come from the salesmen's commission. Everyone was satisfied, primarily because everyone concerned had an opportunity to throw his ideas into the hopper. The plan worked, as indicated by the fact that in 1926 the foremen secured $104,445 worth of business.

It is also interesting that this whole incident was reported in the "Davey Bulletin" in a rather lengthy article headed, "The Commission Battle."

While all of this was going on, there was a different attitude developing about the men who could attend the Davey Institute of Tree Surgery. In place of cajoling men to attend the Institute, they were now carefully selected. The first step was to hire the best men available. Those who were good enough to last a full season were reviewed, and the best of them were invited to come to Kent as students. These men were required to study the Correspondence Course and were given additional training by the foremen before entering the Institute for three terms of intensive instruction.

Some idea of the popularity of the Institute can be gained from the 1925 enrollment figures. There were 280 students and 28 faculty members. It was estimated that the school cost the Company $25,000 for the approximate three month period.

The result of this careful selection and training drew many favorable comments about the high type of men who were employed by Davey and particularly their attitude. Opinions like this were expressed again and again by a number of key executives from Akron banks and industries who had been invited to attend the annual meeting banquet in 1926. They all seemed to be summed up in a statement made by C. B. Raymond, who at that time was Board Chairman of B. F. Goodrich Company, who said, "I was indeed surprised to see the size of your organization and was much impressed by its wonderful spirit and enthusiasm."

In addition to comments like the one from C. B. Raymond, there was recognition from other important sectors of the business community. In 1924, a year after his death, John Davey was listed third in the book, "Fifty Famous Farmers." It was published by Macmillan and Company.

Further indication of the growing interest and recognition of Tree Surgery happened in 1925 when three newsreel companies, Pathe, International and Fox took movies of "Biff" Staples and his crew working in New York's Central Park. The films were shown in theaters all over the United States.

The spirit and enthusiasm of the Davey organization was built and maintained by a thoughtful management. There were a number of employee benefits, all offered to make the Company a good place to work. In 1925 another benefit was added. It was a bonus plan of five cents an hour. The number of bonus hours was computed on the actual time worked, from the close of the annual convention to the end of the Northern season, when the bonus was paid. It was one more way the Company found to say, "Thank you" to its workers.

A generous action taken by Martin in 1926 serves as another indication that he had an interest in trees and conservation which transcended just the commercial aspects. In that year, he announced the Martin L. Davey Forest Conservation Essay Contest. The prize was a $4,000 scholarship to be paid at the rate of $1,000 per year to any Ohio College or University. The Federation of Women's Clubs endorsed the idea and took over the responsibility for running it. Miles A. Smith, a young man of 18, was declared the winner and chose to attend Ohio State University.

A project which drew a great deal of favorable attention to the Company, occurred during the same year. The Sesquicentennial was being held in Philadelphia. The annual convention of the American Legion

The Sesquicentennial celebration in Philadelphia in 1926 where Martin Davey arranged for the planting of thirteen trees for the thirteen original states.

was being held that Fall in the same city. Martin conceived the idea that a substantial patriotic contribution could be made by planting thirteen trees on the grounds of Independence Hall to commemorate the thirteen original states.

Detailed preparations were made for the event to make it an elaborate affair. The Governors of the original states were invited to attend. Most of them accepted or saw to it that their state was represented by an official delegate. The ceremony was planned to take place during the Legion Convention. The National Commander and other officers offered gracious cooperation. Other national patriotic societies were invited to send their officials. These included: The Daughters of the American Revolution; Colonial Dames; Sons of the American Revolution and several organizations growing out of the Civil War period.

Soil from each state had been gathered and carefully packaged and labeled so that the roots of the trees could be planted in soil from the state it was to honor.

The event developed into a gala affair. A luncheon was held for the more than two hundred dignitaries that were present. A big parade was scheduled which included men on horses, drum and bugle corps, marching societies, motorcycle police and automobiles to carry the dig-

Learning the job at the Davey School in the late 20s.

nitaries. The parade route went through the heart of the city and was viewed by thousands of people.

The trees were planted with appropriate ceremony. As a final gesture the trees were taken care of by the Davey Company for several years at its own expense, to be sure they would grow and flourish.

While the planting of the commemorative trees was a patriotic gesture, it symbolized an important part of Martin Davey's success; the ability to think big and to apply a large measure of creative ability to solve all kinds of problems.

A typical example of the creative ability used to solve problems is provided by a course of action taken by Bob McIver, during the 1925-26 school term.

McIver, who had been a Foreman and Assistant Chief Expert, was teaching in the Institute that year. It was February, and when he faced the problem of giving the class instruction on practical tree surgery, there was two feet of snow on the ground. It looked like an impossible task but he came up with an inventive solution. He rented the first floor and basement of the Lutz building in Kent, then proceeded to build an inside forest. On each level he erected four rows with twelve, floor to ceiling tree sections in each. They were firmly anchored to the floor and held up at the top with a system of ingenious braces.

The ability to improvise and to find inventive solutions to problems was a hallmark of Davey men. While it was true there were certain principles and methods which needed to be precisely followed in practicing their profession, there were times when ingenuity was needed, because no two assignments were ever exactly the same. This ability was demonstrated by Bob McIver in building his inside forest.

Sometimes the creative ability of the tree men was not solely confined to business. Skits and presentations were a standard procedure with every graduating class of the Institute. Even original lyrics were written for class songs. On occasion, serious business was combined with a light touch, like the Christmas Tree the sales force set up in the home office for Martin in 1926. In place of the usual ornaments, new orders were hung on the tree. In the first eleven days, 253 of these "ornaments" arrived in Kent to be hung on the branches. Enough orders were secured to set a new record for December volume.

The December sales success was a forecast of what was to come. Sales for 1927 reached $2,400,000. While it took from 1909 to 1924 to reach the magic million dollar mark, it took just two years to add the second million. Each year exceeded the previous year's performance. From the $1,200,000 in 1924 the figures moved up to $1,600,000 in 1925, $2,000,000 in 1926 and $2,400,000 in 1927. The numbers spoke a language of their own which translated into one word . . . "Success."

All of the public attention Davey was getting, the growing reputation and expanded volume, soon caught the eye of Wall Street. In 1927 Hornblower and Weeks approached Martin with a proposal to make a public offering of Davey Tree Expert Company stock. Martin refused the offer in the following letter written in response to the offer:

> "While I appreciate your inquiry, I must be frank in saying that we have no desire or reason to sell any portion of the Davey Company, except to our own employees. We have a peculiar pride in the development of a business which renders a high order of service to the tree-owning public. The quality of service and technique and personnel which we have built into this institution as well as the steady upward progress of the profession which we represent can only be maintained by the active management of those who own it. For the benefit of our business and its future, we should much prefer to have a portion of the stock held by our responsible employees who have helped to build the institution, and who ought to have an opportunity to share in the profits."

The reputation the Davey Tree Expert Company earned for high quality work was expressed by an experience which occurred in 1928. At the time Davey was doing some line clearing for the Fulton Light, Heat and Power Company of Fulton, New York. Tree owners always seemed pleased when they knew Davey men were to trim their trees for power lines. Capitalizing on this attitude, the Superintendent of the power company offered that if any resident along the right of way had trees with minor diseases, he would have Davey Tree Surgeons treat them and the utility would pay the bill.

Martin, Paul and all of Davey management realized that the fine reputation the Company enjoyed was due in a large measure to the people who were associated with it. Management tried to reward its most outstanding people by promoting them to greater levels of responsibility whenever it was possible.

"Biff" Staples was one of these. In 1928 he was promoted to Chief Expert of Tree Moving in the Western area. In making the promotion, management stated "that it was in recognition of his expertise and years of service to the Company."

"Biff" joined the Company in 1915. He attended the Institute and taught in it. He was the first line clearing expert and was one of the first to become engaged in large tree moving. Biff also was a member of Paul Davey's research staff. Even after his retirement, he continues to write a tree column for "Flower and Garden," a magazine devoted to the interests of the serious amateur gardener.

Another of these men, who was a tower of strength over the years, was David Quincy Grove. He joined the Davey Tree Expert Company in 1910 and retired in June of 1950. He was the first Chief Expert for the Company, the first Chief Supervisor and the first field man to be picked as a Director of the Company. During his forty year career, Grove made many important contributions to the progress of the Davey Tree Expert Company. He created, then helped to maintain uniform field policies. He also established an approved list of standardized procedures and methods for tree surgery. Both of these helped to build and maintain the high and uniform quality of performance for which Davey has always been so well known. He took the Company slogan, "Do it right or not at all," seriously . . . and bent every effort to make it come alive.

Myrna Smith (nee Young) was another person who played an important role in the affairs of the Davey Tree Expert Company. She joined the Company in 1919 . . . although not quite seventeen years old at the time, she had already finished high school and was launched on a career that would continue until she retired in 1964. In March of 1926 she married Barton H. Smith, a valuable and trusted Davey employee. The couple have one son, born in 1930.

It wasn't long after Myrna Smith joined the Company, that her industry and proficiency were apparent and recognized by her superiors.

But the best testimony regarding her value, is found in the unpublished memoirs of Martin L. Davey.

He had this to say about her, "On the basis of known merit, I must say in simple fairness that Mrs. Myrna Smith has been one of the most valuable persons connected with me in business and politics. In addition to the brilliance of her mind, she has been a prodigious worker and has carried an immense load of responsibility for many years with an apparent ease and willingness. The things I have admired most about her, however, have been her unqualified loyalty and integrity."

Mrs. Smith participated in Martin Davey's congressional campaign of 1920 and in every campaign which followed. According to Martin she developed a rare aptitude for politics and showed great understanding. After each campaign she would resume her work with the Davey Tree Expert Company until she went to Columbus to become Martin's official secretary when he became Governor of Ohio. After Martin left the Governor's office, Mrs. Smith resumed her career with the Davey Tree Expert Company. Later on she became a Director of the Company.

In mentioning these, or other individuals it is not with the intent of implying that they were the only ones who made important contributions to the Company's growth. Rather, they are pointed out as being typical of a large group of men and women who spent their whole careers with the Davey Tree Expert Company. Every one of them played an important part in the success the Company enjoyed.

It took a large number of people to carry on the Davey business of Tree Surgery. In 1929 the Company had over a thousand people on its payroll. In that year the business volume reached $3,250,000.

It seemed as if all the dreams and hard work and sacrifice were paying off. But often people in the midst of the struggle forget the ingredients that went into the formula for success. It is often left to outsiders to offer an accurate analysis. In the case of Davey, it was done by Phil Kelley, who enjoyed a national reputation as a business man. At the time of his observation, he was Advertising Manager of the B. F. Goodrich Company. He stated that in his opinion, there were six points that accounted for the Davey success.

> "1. Davey men are selected by a careful recruiting process.
> 2. The work offers a field of specialization without monotony because no two assignments are alike.
> 3. There exists a real pride of craftsmanship.
> 4. The functions are based on a sound philosophy.
> 5. It's a profession which requires thought.
> 6. All of these were the result of aggressive leadership which was the driving force to bring all of these things into existence and then to create a service that added to the world's beauty by saving trees."

In spite of the many kudos offered by people like Phil Kelley, which in large part sprang from the success the Company was enjoying during the great days of the Twenties, there were signs appearing that the economy was overheating to the extent that it was due to boil over.

Then it happened. The stock market crashed in October of 1929. People who were rich on paper, found that in a matter of hours, they were paupers. The stock market crash and other indications were harbingers of things to come.

There was no immediate effect on the Davey Company. But all too soon, it and all business were to be in for some trying times.

XV   The Economy
Plummets

The momentous and violent crash of the stock market in 1929 did not have an immediate effect on the Davey Tree Expert Company. Sales records show a volume of over three million dollars for that year. Other actions taken by the Company indicated that the management was looking forward to continued growth and prosperity. A greatly expanded advertising program was approved. It included a network radio program which was covered in an earlier chapter. This was also the time the Davey Compressor Company was founded.

There appeared to be sound justification for the management's optimism. Davey Tree business for the first half of 1930 showed a husky twenty percent gain over the previous year. Martin felt that a large part of this increase was due to results from the radio program.

But, by July, another kind of performance was starting to take shape. During that month business was off eight percent from a year earlier. Other parts of the business sector were showing similar results. It was apparent that the whole economy was in a down hill slide. No one was quite sure how serious the condition was or what to expect of the future. The initial reaction of most business men was to keep up a bold front by optimistically proclaiming their faith in the basic strength of the economy. This posture was encouraged by President Hoover and the people around him.

But the signs of depression were all too clear as far as Davey was concerned. The sudden change in the Company's performance was a warning that could not be ignored, particularly in light of the fact that all business appeared to be suffering the same kind of experience. Martin was very troubled by these conditions which were so general and wide spread. He thought about this problem very earnestly and upon returning from a trip to New York decided to cut expenses drastically.

This is one of the few times he made a major decision without discussing it with others, or informing them of his plans. He recognized that this was a matter of extreme emergency and for that reason a decision could not wait for prolonged debate to arrive at an agreement. He immediately cut $275,000 out of yearly expenses.

While this was a shocking cutback, particularly after years of growth, Martin later regretted that he didn't reduce expenses even more at the time he made these initial reductions. He pointed out that he might have cut the radio program from six months to three and other advertising could have been reduced or eliminated . . . all things which had to be done eventually.

Following 1930, business conditions went from bad to worse through 1932. Every spring would witness a mild upturn; only to be followed by a more severe decline in the fall.

In 1931 President Hoover was trying to bolster the morale of the country. He made his famous announcement, "Prosperity is just around the corner." Those words taunted him for many years. He tried to change the economic trend by asking heads of large corporations to carry on at full speed; to augment their repair, expansion and replacement programs.

Nothing seemed to help. The roots of the depression ran too deep. Agriculture was in severe distress. Thousands of farms were sold out under the eyes of their owners. People were losing their homes, unable to keep up the mortgage payments. Business failures increased dramatically. Buying power was shrinking fast.

The pressures on Martin were severe and seemed to be coming from every direction at once. He had been the Democratic candidate for Governor of Ohio in 1928. Although he was defeated during the Republican landslide victory of that year, he ran 514,000 votes ahead of his ticket, which had been headed by Al Smith, the Democrats' nominee for President. Because of this Martin's political influence with voters of the state was well recognized, which resulted in party leaders and others urging him to again become a candidate for Governor in 1930. He had also started to make some very substantial personal investments in Kent real estate. The radio program was taking a large share of his time. The affairs of the Davey Tree Expert Company were requiring a great deal of his personal attention. For the first time he admitted he was tired.

After considering all of the demands being made upon him, Martin decided that he would devote the major portion of his energy to the Davey Tree Expert Company. This meant that he would forego seeking public office for the time being. He reasoned that the Company to which he had devoted nearly twenty-five years of his life was the most important of all of the enterprises in which he was involved. The business provided not only his livelihood, but that of his entire family, to say nothing of the hundreds of loyal employees who looked to Davey for a paycheck.

This was a wise decision on Martin's part. The next three years were to be the most difficult in the history of the Davey Tree Expert Company. Volume of the Company dropped from more than $3,000,000 in 1930 to about $2,000,000 in 1931 then plummeted to $700,000 in 1932 . . . less than twenty-five percent of what it had been two years earlier.

Each drop in volume meant a corresponding cut in expenses. Martin pointed out that, "Just when it appeared we had cut everything possible, we found we had to do it all over again."

When business goes down that rapidly, it's almost impossible to adjust operating expenses at the same rate of speed. As a result, profits were something that happened in the past and the Company was having the unpleasant experience of sharp losses.

The determinations of where and what to cut were difficult for Davey management. By this time they knew they were fighting for the very life of their business. The Company continued the radio program and the resident school during the winter of 1931-1932. Then both fell victim to the economic cutbacks.

In 1932, for the first time in many years, the Company was unable to pay off the bank loans at the end of the season. It was indebted to the First Central Trust Company of Akron, The Guardian Trust Company of Cleveland and The Cleveland Trust Company for a total of about $250,000. The amount spent for the school and the advertising program for the '31-'32 season was about equal to the bank loans.

When the Company found itself unable to pay back the banks at the end of the season, it seemed quite natural that the banks should scrutinize the Company's situation more closely than previously.

The banks advanced a modest amount of credit at the beginning of 1932 based on a good past record. Business the first part of that year was considerably better than the previous fall. But, by the early part of the summer, it showed a sharp decline. It was then that the bankers asked the Company to assign its accounts receivable to one of them as trustee for the group. The Company readily agreed because its management believed that borrowed money should be paid back faithfully and as quickly as possible.

The economy was bad, but it was headed for worse times which would reflect on the affairs of the Davey Tree Expert Company.

On February 12, 1933, Martin and Paul were in New York trying to negotiate some business for the Davey Compressor Company. Martin had bought a New York newspaper and as he glanced through it, he saw an article announcing that the Governor of Michigan had closed all State Banks. He turned to Paul and asked him his opinion. He replied, "I think we are going to be in for some real trouble." Unfortunately, his forecast was much too accurate.

Banks in other states closed in rapid succession. Franklin D. Roosevelt had been elected President. The period between February 12th and his inauguration on March 4th, 1933, has been regarded as one of the bleakest in the economic history of the United States. Roosevelt's first step after taking office was to close *all* banks, then to open those which were solvent, first in the big cities, then in medium sized communities and finally those in the smallest towns.

The Davey Tree Expert Company had all of its cash in two of the banks which failed to open. As a consequence, the Company found itself in dire straits. It had a reasonable amount of accounts receivable, but, as checks came in, no bank would give credit for them until they had cleared to be sure they were good. The only cash in sight was $10,000 in Canada. Martin sent William R. Williams and the Kent Chief of Police to get that money. The exchange rate was so low, they got only $8,200 in American funds.

Money was so tight there wasn't enough to meet the payroll. Martin wrote to all of the employees and told them in a straightforward manner exactly the kind of problem the Company was facing.

The response from the Davey workers was one of the few bright spots during those dark days. Many said they had local credit and could get by for several weeks without paychecks. Others asked for five or six dollars a week and said, "we will get along somehow." People in the home office were put on half pay. The salesmen didn't ask for any draw, and when they needed a few dollars apologized for asking.

Martin wrote to all of the companies to which money was owed and explained his company's predicament. He pointed out that Davey had always paid its bills promptly in the past and asked for understanding and cooperation during the present crisis. He also took pains to point out that the Davey Tree Expert Company would work out of its present problems and would continue to be a good customer. In response some of the creditors said they understood and would cooperate; others said they found themselves in the same condition and replied, "Send money as soon as you can."

To keep the business afloat, Martin borrowed all the cash possible from members of the family. These loans even included money from his wife's personal bank account. Paul came up with some money advanced from the meager funds of the Davey Compressor Company.

Members of the Davey family made other financial sacrifices in the way of salaries to make more money available to run the business.

After the bank holiday the business situation got brighter. The Davey Company business picked up rapidly. In three months the field payroll was four times as great as it had been in March. The employees had all received their back pay, but the money owed to the family and the bankers had to wait a while longer.

In April of 1933 there was a burst of optimism. Unfortunately it was rather short lived. By September of that year, Davey management was again forced to retrench. A number of jobs were combined and whenever possible employees were transferred to other positions . . . some were sent to the Davey Compressor Company and some were returned to jobs that were available with the field force. But the time finally came when the Company was faced with the necessity of laying-off a number of valuable employees, a decision that was hard to reach and even more difficult to carry out.

During the time of what appeared to be a roller coaster course of the economy, the Federal Government was almost frantic in its attempts to level it out. Roosevelt set up the NRA in an effort to get business to pull itself up by its boot straps. Martin, in expressing his opinion of this said, "The president failed to recognize that too many business organizations had lost so much money during the extremely hard times, that they were much like the man who had lost too much blood . . . they were too weak to carry on in a normal manner."

In a further attempt to bolster the economy, the Federal Government established several relief programs in the fall of 1933. W.P.A. was one of those, and its purpose was to provide jobs by instituting a massive public works program. While the basic intent of the program was probably a good one, actually W.P.A. had a damaging effect on some individuals and companies. The Davey Tree Expert Company was one of those being hurt by this new Federal program.

A large part of the public works program was being done in parks, which of course included trimming trees. The relief administration began to hire trained Davey Tree Surgeons to supervise the work. The Government was paying a dollar and twenty cents per hour, while the average being paid by Davey was seventy cents. No one could blame the men for taking the higher rate of pay, even though the government jobs, at best, would be of limited duration. As a result Davey was in danger of losing many of its most valuable men.

In this emergency, Martin phoned F. A. Bartlett, the head of Davey's chief competitor and asked what his experience was in losing men to the government. Bartlett informed him that his company was losing men so fast in this period that he was afraid of what the consequences might be.

It seemed to Martin that the only way out of this dilemma was to see someone at the top of the government . . . if possible, the President. He felt that this was the only way that some modification of the program would be made to enable companies like Davey and Bartlett to stay in business. Acting on this theory, Martin made arrangements to meet Bartlett in Washington.

They arrived in Washington on a Monday morning. Martin, of course, knew his way around official circles because of the many years he had spent in the city as a Congressman. Due to this past experience, he was able to arrange to see the President's Secretary, Marvin McIntyre. Martin asked to see Roosevelt for a brief meeting. He was told that it was impossible. However, Martin persisted and finally said, "Mr. Secretary, this is a case of must. We *have* to see the President, even though it be very brief, it's a matter of life and death for our companies. We will simply have to stay here until we can see him."

Finally, after much urging, McIntyre consulted his engagement book and said, "Well, if you can wait until Friday, I can get you in for one minute at one o'clock." The two men grasped at the straw with alacrity. Martin was convinced that if they could get the President's attention long enough for him to understand what the relief program was doing to both of their companies, some immediate action would be taken to remedy the situation.

This, of course, meant that the two men had to stay in Washington from Monday to Friday. The big problem was to explain the situation to

President Roosevelt in as few words as possible and be impressive enough to make him want to take some corrective action. One minute . . . sixty seconds . . . wasn't very long to get done what they felt they had to do.

Some idea about the limitation placed on them can be gathered from the fact that a trained radio announcer can speak a hundred and forty words in a minute. One hundred and forty words, at the most, to make the most important sales presentation either of these men would ever be called upon to make! Martin and Bartlett spent their time trying to find ways they could make the most effective presentation of their case. Somehow the "big idea" or the "grabber" kept eluding them. After many hours of wrestling with the problem, a dramatic idea occurred to Martin.

Before the big idea could be used, the two men put in their time the best way they could, waiting for a Friday that seemed as if it would never arrive. On the fateful day they arranged to be at the White House a full half hour before their one o'clock appointment, to be sure they would not miss their opportunity. One o'clock came and passed. There was a steady stream of individuals and groups in and out of the President's office. Martin started to be concerned that, because it was getting close to the President's lunch time, they might be put off. At last, at one forty-five, McIntyre beckoned to them, and said they might see the President, but warned them, two or three times, that it was to be, "just for one minute."

Martin and the President had met before so they exchanged brief greetings after which Mr. Bartlett was presented. Martin then opened the conversation with the attention-getting idea which had occurred to him earlier in the week. It went something like this, "Mr. President, if you were on an errand of mercy and your car struck a man, would you take him to the hospital?"

The President replied, "Certainly. What's your trouble?"

This gave the two men the opportunity to tell him that the emergency relief program was hiring their men away from them by paying wages they couldn't possibly afford.

Roosevelt asked what their average rate was and he was told, "About seventy cents an hour, while the government was paying one dollar and twenty cents for the same men." He replied, "We shouldn't be doing that; it isn't right."

Then Martin said, "Mr. President, if this policy continues, every company like ours and Mr. Bartlett's will be out of business by spring. Then who is going to hire these men, when the government is through with them?"

"Well, that is something to think about," he answered. He then turned to his secretary and said, "Marvin, I wish you would call Harry Hopkins and arrange an appointment with him for these men. And tell him to find a solution." From the standpoint of the two men the most important words the President said were, "Find a solution."

The appointment with Hopkins was arranged for the same day in the late afternoon. He followed the President's instructions "to find a solution." After discussing the problem at some length, an agreement was reached whereby the Government would pay eighty cents an hour against the Companies' rate of seventy cents. The two men agreed that this would not be an unfair arrangement.

Most important from the standpoint of Davey and Bartlett, it meant the saving of their companies. To their employees, it meant they would have jobs and would not be out of work and on relief by the end of the winter. Obviously, the men working for the two companies would be better off.

Unfortunately, even this dramatic action did not completely correct the situation in which Davey found himself. The business was at a low ebb in the fall of 1933. Volume was down, and as a result, the Company was hurting financially. Also it was still in debt to the closed banks and its condition did not warrant credit from any other source.

In the years preceding the Depression, the Company had instituted a carefully planned program of steadily increasing the corporate life insurance on Martin's life. By the early Thirties this amounted to $800,000. During the prosperous years the insurance had accumulated a substantial cash or loan value. Over the years the Company had borrowed against it rather heavily. The amount of the loans was so large and the interest charges so heavy, the management decided to cancel half the policies and lighten the burden by reducing the premiums and the interest charges. This meant surrendering the oldest policies which had the largest loans against them leaving $400,000 worth of corporate insurance with annual premiums of $18,000 plus the interest charges on the remaining loans.

By 1934 the affairs of the Davey Tree Expert Company were improved to the point where Martin felt he could yield to the pressure of those who wanted him to seek political office. He decided to enter the race for the Governorship of Ohio. He was elected after the 1934 pri

116

mary and general election. But his decision to run for office had near disastrous results for the Davey Tree Expert Company.

The trouble occurred in June during the primary campaign. Martin had been in New York where he had received two excellent contracts for the Company. On his way home he stopped off at Coshocton, Ohio where he received a message to contact his secretary. She informed him that the bankers to whom the Company was still in debt had left an urgent message saying that they wanted an immediate meeting with Martin. He asked her to contact the men and told her to tell them that it would be impossible to see them immediately because he had committed himself to a series of meetings which he could not cancel. He asked her to call the men and tell them he would contact them as soon as possible to arrange a satisfactory meeting date. All of this seemed rather high handed, but Martin had become aware of a change in the banker's attitude since he had entered the primary campaign. He had also learned that the bankers wanted to take away the salary he was being paid by the tree company because of his political activity.

The meeting date was arranged and held in the offices of the closed Guardian Trust Company in Cleveland. The three banks involved were: First Central Trust Company of Akron, The Guardian Trust Company of Cleveland (both of these were closed), and the Cleveland Trust Company, which had remained open. Each bank had an officer representing it at the meeting. As the meeting opened the atmosphere was rather tense. None of the bankers seemed to want to open the subject. So, after about a half an hour wasted in small talk, Martin became impatient and said, "Gentlemen, why are we here?" The chairman of the meeting started to hem and haw and appeared to be evading the issue. Martin then decided to face it head on by saying, "Gentlemen, I understand you want to take away the salary paid to me by the Davey Tree Expert Company." The chairman replied, "What would you say, if we said yes to that?"

Martin shot back with, "That would be the damnedest, rottenest treatment one man could give to another."

By this time Martin was seething. He continued by saying, "You men propose to take the bread out of my family's mouth and that's something you, or no one else, is going to do. You have the power to put our Company through the wringer, but you would be damned fools to do it. If you want to take such drastic actions, you can take what you can get and go to hell. What you would get would be a small amount after paying our current accounts. You can have the office furniture and the typewriters and I will take the men and start a new business. They know me, but they don't know you."

He continued his attack by saying, "Gentlemen, I am your best bet. In fact, I am your only bet. If you have good sense you will play ball with me. I have never defaulted on an obligation in my life, and I don't propose to fail on this one. Your only chance of getting your money is through me, unless you want to make perfect damned fools of yourselves, you will cooperate with me in my effort to make our business prosper and pay what we owe. You can take it or leave it."

A heavy silence followed this outburst. After a few minutes which seemed like hours, with no one saying a word, the chairman of the meeting turned to Mr. Stansberry, who represented the Cleveland Trust Company and asked for his opinion. He replied promptly and with some emphasis. "Why certainly this man should be paid his salary. Whoever thought of not doing so was very unwise." The others very quickly agreed.

Then the question arose about if, and when, the tree company should pay back the money borrowed from Martin's wife and other members of the Davey family. Again, Mr. Stansberry spoke up and expressed the opinion that these were both legal and moral obligations and should be paid before the banks got their money. The others went along without a sign of dissent. They appeared to be only too happy to get the embarrassing situation out of the way without any further argument.

True to his word, Martin saw to it that the bank loans were paid off during the next two and a half years. An interesting side light is that Davey paid off the full amount due. A great many other companies made deals to pay off their obligations at a discount.

After Martin was elected Governor, Paul took over many of the responsibilities of General Manager. Each week he would travel to Columbus and review the Company's affairs with Martin, who continued as President of the Davey Tree Expert Company.

Business continued to improve but the mix was changing rapidly. The largest volume was coming from line clearing assignments for telephone and power companies. Spraying and tree moving were also becoming important segments of the business. Both line clearing and tree moving could be done during the winter months, which helped to level out the Northern season.

There was an increasing number of foremen who were buying cars and using them in the business. Many of them also bought trailers through the Company. These were used to haul tools and equipment to the jobs and to take away brush and debris after assignments were finished. It was about this time that Paul Hershey decided to use a pick-up truck. It proved to be such a useful vehicle that others soon followed his lead. The Company paid the foremen for the use of their cars, trucks and trailers by the hours of use, through an expense account arrangement.

These were difficult years . . . the kind no one wants to go through again. The Davey Company survived, while many other companies went out of business. But Davey's survival was due to a combination of qualities; strong leadership, loyal employees, courage, creativeness and a firm belief in themselves and the purpose for which they were organized.

It was during the darkest days and after coming through a particularly harrowing experience that Martin was moved to comment, "Adversity seems to draw people more closely together and makes them stronger in the process."

The annual Christmas tree which the Davey Company arranged for many years at the former Sterling, Linder, Davis department store in Cleveland.

XVI   Adventure, The Other Side of Tree Surgery

The time from 1929 to 1934 could easily be compared to a ride down a turbulent, white water river; shooting rapids, avoiding rocks that could wreck and sink the craft. Then rounding a bend and encountering a quiet pool, that offered a respite from the threats of destruction.

So it must have seemed to Martin and his management, as they fought valiantly to avoid the economic rocks of destruction that threatened the very life of their business. There were also pools of tranquility, events which were much less turbulent than those in which management found themselves engaged. While some of these activities may appear common place, they played an important role in shaping the future and character of the Davey Tree Expert Company.

Even in the most troubled times, Davey Tree Surgeons experienced adventures that were peculiarly their own. Sometimes when they were called upon to treat very old trees important events were revealed. Often they would find bullets imbedded in trees, reminders of battles fought many years before.

One of the more interesting discoveries came about in 1929, when Davey Tree Surgeons were working on an assignment to remove a huge elm, in a small Massachusetts town. As the men were working, they discovered the roots were growing on the top of some granite blocks, which had the appearance of a building foundation. Further exploration led to finding fragments of handpressed bricks. It was found out later, that these had been imported from England, early in the seventeenth century. The annual rings of the stump indicated that the tree was about a hundred and sixty years old, which meant it was planted before the

Revolution. Additional inquiry revealed that this was the site of the first free public school building in America.

Other discoveries were of a more personal nature. These were brought about by the travel of tree surgeons, necessitated by the far flung operations of the Davey Tree Expert Company. There were reports of men who saw Yellowstone National Park for the first time, while on their way to work amidst the grandeur of the great Northwest. They talked about the satisfaction of working in Washington, D. C., on trees that surrounded important buildings and on others that were growing in famous locations in the nation's capital. There was still an almost endless stream of men who crossed the Hudson and saw, for the first time, the beauty of the Hudson Valley, where Martin had enjoyed his initial success in the tree surgery business. Others encountered the pleasure of working in the South, escaping the discomfort of a Northern winter. Time after time men wrote and expressed the happiness these experiences provided them. Many of their letters appeared in the Davey Bulletin. The opportunity to travel and see the world was one of the benefits which attracted men to the Davey Tree Expert Company.

It was also during the early Thirties that the direction in which the Company was headed, took a slightly different course than had been evident previously. There was more and more emphasis placed on the newer services, like tree moving, spraying and line clearing.

In other action, the Davey Investment Company was founded in 1930. It was organized with Martin as President and Treasurer, Paul Davey and Roy H. Smith (father of Alexander M. Smith) Vice-Presidents and Wesley O. Hollister as Secretary. Holdings of that company were quite substantial and included two large land developments, an apartment, several business blocks and a number of houses.

During this same time, it was decided to incorporate the Canadian company. On November fifth, 1930, letters of patents were issued by Canadian authorities and the company became known as Davey Tree Expert Company, Ltd.

Shortly after the incorporation of the Canadian Company, W. O. Hollister traveled to Toronto to make arrangements to purchase material and supplies from Canadian manufacturers to be used in Canada. This action emphasized the fact that Davey intended to be an important part of the Canadian business community.

Martin was now the President of four companies; the Davey Tree Expert Company, the Davey Compressor Company, Davey Tree Expert Company, Ltd. and the Davey Investment Company. He also finally was an important figure in a fifth company, the City Bank of Kent. Of all of the things Martin had done in business, this one was the most frustrating experience.

It all came about rather innocently. In 1930 Martin had been invited to become a Director of the City Bank. He knew nothing of the bank's condition, but since it was considered something of an honor to be elected a director of a bank, he accepted. He soon discovered that the bank was in trouble due to action of its principal stockholder. This man had borrowed $105,000 from the bank on unsecured loans. To make matters worse, he had pledged his City Bank stock with the Guardian Trust Company of Cleveland, for a loan of $80,000. He was in debt to several other banks, and to personal friends, including Martin, who had loaned him $10,000. The only visible asset this man appeared to have was stock of rather questionable value. He had some valuable real estate, but it, too, was encumbered with a first and second mortgage, totaling $200,000.

The man was unable to do anything towards paying off these loans. He was unable to pay even the interest. As a result the Guardian Trust foreclosed and took over his bank stock. Since the law prohibited one bank from owning stock in another, the Guardian Trust approached Martin and asked him to buy it. They offered to sell him the $80,000 worth of stock for $50,000. Martin hesitated. At the time, he owned less than $7,000 worth of City Bank shares. In fact, he toyed with the idea of selling that small interest and getting out of the situation. However, he realized that if he did, it would indicate a lack of confidence in the institution, which would hurt it.

Meantime, Martin and others in the bank were trying to do whatever they could to save their principal shareholder from bankruptcy and taking the institution down with him. To further complicate matters, a story appeared in July of 1930, in the Cleveland papers, that a man of the same name had gone bankrupt. The resulting confusion caused a mild run on the bank. Martin was out of town when this took place. His associates contacted him immediately and secured his permission to release a statement to the effect that he was taking over the bank.

The president of one of the banks to which the man in trouble was indebted, took over his stock at $1 per share. The City Bank bought his real estate for two hundred thousand dollars then sold it to the Davey Investment Company for two hundred and fifty thousand dollars. The extra fifty thousand went to the City Bank to help wipe out some of the man's bad paper.

All of this action took place in the late summer of 1931. If the Depression had not become worse, these steps would undoubtedly have saved the bank. After the nationwide bank holiday, the City Bank had permission to re-open. It was unable to do so . . . because all of its funds were tied up in banks which remained closed.

About three years of hard work went for naught. In reviewing this experience, Martin said, "If I had sold my stock when I first learned that the bank was in trouble, I would have saved myself a lot of worry and money." The City Bank, after several years paid off every depositor.

While Martin was trying to save the bank, the Davey Tree Company was having its own problems. In 1932 it showed a loss of $185,000. The next year, the loss was reduced to $25,000, then by 1934, the Company was able, once again to show a profit. Although the profit for that year was only a meager $3,700, it was encouraging to management, indicating that the Company was headed in the right direction.

While the Davey Company was staging a come back, during those troubled years, business overall left a great deal to be desired. For instance, in a great industrial state like Ohio, twenty percent of its people were on relief in 1935. At this time, the Davey Company success came from capitalizing on the opportunities offered by some of the newer services which had been initiated in the Twenties. One of these was Line Clearing. It moved from $63,000 in 1933 to $389,000 in 1935. Other services, like Spraying and Tree Moving, also made substantial progress which helped to produce a total volume for 1935 of $960,000.

While all of the new services were becoming of increasing importance to the Company, they did require substantial investments in equipment and materials. As early as 1930 the Company had a fleet of forty truck-mounted spray units. Tree moving used heavy trucks and specially built trailers, all of which called for a substantial investment. Also by 1935, the Company had ten warehouses scattered across the country. They were located in Ohio, Georgia, Texas, Michigan, New York, Connecticut, Missouri, Indiana, Pennsylvania and Canada.

These new services called for special training of the men. As was indicated earlier, tree moving was a specialized operation, requiring special knowledge of trees and the heavy equipment used in moving them. Line clearing also called for special instruction. A unique method for teaching the skill necessary for this operation was developed by Frans F. Lofgren, in 1931, when he built a scale model for class room use. It consisted of miniature power poles with wires strung through trees constructed to the same scale. This model gave students the opportunity to actually perform the sort of shaping operations they would later be required to do when engaged in line clearing. Mr. Lofgren became Sales Manager of the company some 20 years later.

Even during the trying days of the Thirties, outstanding records were being set. One of these came about in 1933, which involved an assignment requiring the use of 55,700 gallons of spray material, to fight canker worm on the 400 acre farm estate of E. F. Pierce who raised blooded Guernsey dairy cattle. This was the largest amount of spray material used on a single job, up to that time. This project was another that demonstrated the dedication Davey men gave to their jobs. During the assignment, constant winds interfered with the spraying operation. In order to combat the situation, crew members got up at 3:30 in the morning to lay down their material before the winds started to blow at 5:30 A.M.

Although spraying was a lucrative part of the business, Davey continued to promote the importance of birds as allies to fight tree destroying insects. In a round-up of scientific literature, considerable space was devoted to the protection of "our feathered friends." Also for a number of years, the Davey Bulletin carried a column on the importance of birds in the natural environment.

There were a number of interesting experiences during the Thirties associated with big tree moving. The Davey Tree Expert Company was called upon, on numerous occasions, to move large trees to provide natural shade and beauty for expositions and trade fairs. One of these was an assignment in 1933 when the Company was called upon to plant twenty-nine elms on the grounds of the World's Fair, celebrating Chicago's hundredth anniversary.

One of the more unusual tree moving assignments was for a department store in Cleveland, The Sterling and Welch Company, later to become Sterling-Linder-Davis. The task was to supply a live Christmas tree, four stories high, to be displayed inside the store during the Christmas shopping season. The first assignment began in 1935 and was carried on until the store discontinued business in the Nineteen-Sixties. Finding suitable trees for the store often meant hauling one to Cleveland from several hundred miles away. Over the years thousands of people, from all over northern Ohio, came to view and admire those spectacular, beautifully trimmed trees. The visits became a family tradition, like the children's annual trek to see Santa Claus. There were a number of other special assignments involving supplying and trimming large Christmas trees, even to supplying trees for inside the White House.

Following the successful campaign of November, 1934, which saw Martin elected Governor of Ohio, the Company made an important

change in its table of organization. At the annual meeting of the stockholders held in January of 1935, the directors re-elected Martin President,
Treasurer and General Manager. They then elected Paul Davey to a
newly created post, Executive Vice-President and Assistant General Manager, with power to act for the President in his absence.

*Governor Martin L. Davey being sworn in
by Carl V. Weygandt, Chief Justice of the
Supreme Court of Ohio.*

It was in the following year, 1936, that several of the Davey men
were subjected to a rather harrowing experience. It was caused by the
flood which occurred in the Ohio and Mississippi Valleys. The drama of
it all was revealed in the telegrams received by the Company, from the
men working in the area. One from Salesman Billy White said, "Marooned
in Central City, Kentucky. May be weeks before we can get out. Unable
to contact my foremen, Banta, Steadman or Miller in Paducah. Due to
conditions there, I am concerned for their safety. If you hear from them,
wire me if possible. Mrs. White safe at Crestwood."

Some of the other reports, coming in from men working in the area,
said things like this, "Red Cross put me to work carrying messages and

126

clothing." Another, "I have turned in unusual expenses. None authorized
. . . do not have receipts for everything. Few people were worrying
about receipts when I contracted these expenses, like charges for boats."
Still another, "Worked for Red Cross for two days, thirty six hours without stopping. Raining all the while. Ninety-five percent of city under two
to fourteen feet of water. Thirty-three thousand out of thirty-five thousand people have left Paducah. River at sixty-one feet."

Fortunately there were no casualties among the Davey personnel,
working in the area. Terrible as this experience was, it was just another
in a long list of unusual events, in which Davey men participated, adding
one more chapter to the romance of tree surgery.

While the practice of tree surgery had its own unique character, at
least one of the products used by the men in caring for trees, had a
uniqueness of its own. The product was Daveyite, a specially formulated
coating for the protection of pruning wounds. Although it seemed rather
humble in character, it was quite a sophisticated product and takes special care to manufacture. The basic ingredient is asphalt, but a special
kind, available from only three places in the world: Egypt, Trinidad and

Charles Miller labeling cans of "Daveyite."

from the Wasatch Mountains in Utah. In the 1938 period, Egyptian asphalt cost six hundred dollars per ton, which prohibited its use. In contrast the material from Utah cost sixty-five dollars per ton and that from Trinidad cost even less. Other sources, like oil asphalt are not suitable for a tree coating because they carry a large amount of volatile oils which might be injurious to the tree. Further, they do not stand up under hot weather. It requires a rather complicated process before a suitable coating like Daveyite is ready for use. The Davey Research Department made a number of studies in an attempt to find a better coating. But none was found that could match its fine all around qualities. Over the years, Davey Tree Surgeons have used many thousands of gallons of Daveyite. In 1938 alone, 1,650 gallons were purchased by the Company. There was an attempt to market this coating as a proprietory product, but the effort was soon dropped because it was unprofitable.

The Daveyite inventory alone represented a sizeable investment. The same thing is true of other items of material and equipment. Undoubtedly many of the men wondered why the Company stressed the careful use of even simple equipment like saws and ladders. But it was in these areas where profit-robbing leaks could occur.

In spite of all of the admonitions about the proper care of equipment there was a great deal of it lost through damage of one sort or another. Sometimes this would appear to happen with one kind of equipment, that would make it seem like some type of epidemic. For whatever the reasons, an unusual number of ladders were broken in 1938. In that year, almost nine hundred were returned to Kent. More than two-thirds of them had to be junked, representing a loss of three thousand dollars. To correct the situation, David Q. "Red" Grove, who was in charge of the field force as Chief Expert, decided to publish in the Davey Bulletin the names of the foremen who returned broken ladders to Kent. Apparently the men did not like to receive this kind of publicity, because the situation soon corrected itself. The next year only three hundred ladders were returned.

Saws were another item of equipment that got hard usage. As a result there were a great many of them that had to be sharpened and otherwise repaired. In fact it required the full time of one man, to keep the saws in good condition. In one year he restored 2,577 saws to usefulness. While all of this may seem like unimportant detail, it was paying attention to small items of this kind that enabled the Company to be more profitable.

Even though management kept pressure on employees to conserve equipment and materials, there was a fine relationship that existed be-

Charles Miller filing saws.

tween them. People who worked for the Company were particularly fond of Martin. Their feelings for him were demonstrated through a rather touching gesture in 1939. The employees presented to the State of Ohio, two matching elms, planted at the entrance of the state capital to honor Martin. These trees were removed later when an underground parking garage was built.

In 1938, an event took place that undoubtedly must have pleased Martin a great deal. That year, his son Martin L. Davey, Jr., without urging from his father or family, but entirely on his own initiative, asked for the opportunity to be trained as a Tree Surgeon, in Kent, Ohio. He worked that summer as a field man in the Chicago territory. He joined the Company after he graduated from Yale University in 1940. He eventually became president of the Company, but more of that will be reported later.

In 1940, Martin persuaded the Company to enlarge its Board of Directors from nine to seventeen. The original nine had been directors for a number of years.

They were: Martin L. Davey, President; Paul Davey, Executive Vice-

129

President; James A. G. Davey, Vice-President; Charles L. May, Vice-President; Hugo E. Birkner, Vice-President; Harmon L. Carson, Secretary; David Q. "Red" Grove; William R. Williams; Clifford H. Bissler. The eight new directors included the following men and the dates they joined the Company: E. P. Metcalfe, 1910; Wesley O. Hollister, 1913; Orrin B. Crosser, 1919; Charles E. Fadely, 1919; Donald H. Fowler, 1923; J. Harlan Carson, 1928; Edwin S. Pirtle, 1930; and Martin L. Davey, Jr., 1938.

All of these men were actively engaged in the operating end of the business. In making these additions Martin pointed out that since these men had important roles in making day-to-day operating decisions for the Company, he felt they should have a voice in formulating its policies as well.

By the end of 1940, the Davey Tree Expert Company had re-built its volume back to $2,309,000. This was a substantial comeback from the low of 1933, when the Company sales had sunk to $700,000.

But during the previous four years, beginning in 1936 when Germany sent troops into the Rhineland, Europe was again to smoulder with the threat of war. All too soon the antics of the madman who started it would involve the United States . . . and the Davey Tree Expert Company.

XVII The World Is At War

As the Thirties drew to a close, Martin was out of politics. He sought the nomination for Governor in 1938 but was defeated in the primaries by Charles Sawyer. He won the nomination in 1940 but lost the General Election in the Fall of 1940. By this time the economy was improved, so altogether it appeared that the Davey Tree Expert Company might be entering into a period of normal operation, a time when a company could plan for profitable growth.

The decade beginning in 1940 started out normally enough. To be sure there were problems that had to be solved. But there were the challenges that a management faces in operating any business. Some of these were troublesome, like the wage and hour law that established a forty-two hour work week for line clearing crews, and required time and a half for extra hours. Others were of an almost perennial nature and special to the Davey Company. For instance, the Davey Tree Expert Company was a labor-sensitive business which meant that the difference between a good year and an ordinary one often depended on the number of people who could be hired, trained and put into the field.

In 1940, the management of the Company set a goal of hiring three hundred people between the ages of eighteen and twenty years old. This was a much more difficult task than might be imagined. There were some reasons which made this a large order: tree work was hard work; Davey was selective in its hiring practices; and an advantage they offered in the past, no longer existed, the Davey Institute of Tree Surgery, with its promise of professional training. An additional problem was the fact that as the war started to accelerate in Europe, once again the United States became the arsenal for the allies. This meant that there were plenty of jobs available in war related industries, which put one more obstacle in the way of hiring suitable men.

Manpower was not the only shortage that existed. Materials of all kinds were becoming scarce and harder to find. The situation became so bad, that the Davey Company gave Biff Staples the full time job of finding sources for rope, saws, chain, axes, ladders—anything and everything that was necessary for the operation of the business.

There is an interesting story in connection with the way Biff was able to solve the saw shortage. His first move was to gather up all the old junk saws he could find. Some of these were reconditioned and repaired. Others of them were completely remade.

In scrounging around the country looking for material, he visited a mill supply company and in the course of looking through their warehouse, he found a coil of Swedish saw steel. At the time, this discovery was more thrilling than finding gold. He quickly made arrangements to buy the steel, but then ran into another problem, a shortage of saw handles.

He took off to visit the manufacturer of this essential part and tried to buy some, but he was turned down. The reason for the refusal was that there was a shortage of the pear, apple and birch wood, the traditional material from which saw handles had always been made. Biff was not quite willing to accept this as a reason. He stayed around for a couple of days, observing the operation of the company. During the course of his stay, he got an idea, "Why not make saw handles out of plywood?" The manufacturer quickly accepted the idea which provided Davey and others who needed them, an adequate supply of handles. The making, rebuilding and repairing of saws took the full time of two Davey employees, Charlie and Joe Miller.

As 1940 drew to a close, it was far from satisfactory profit-wise. In the midst of these struggles fate struck another blow at the Davey Tree Expert Company.

In the early part of 1941, Martin suffered a severe heart attack, diagnosed as a coronary thrombosis. As a result, although he kept in constant touch with the Company, he was bedridden for several months. It wasn't until the first of the following year that he was able to again take the helm of the Company.

During those months of Martin's illness it was becoming more difficult than ever to find men to staff the crews. The United States was expanding its own preparations for war. The armed services were taking men, others were being siphoned off into war industries at a faster rate than ever before.

On December seventh, 1941, the Japanese launched their sneak attack on Pearl Harbor. Now it appeared that the whole scenario of World War I was to be replayed with the same kind of effect on the Davey Tree Expert Company.

But this time there was to be one important difference. Line clearing was declared an essential activity, necessary to support the war effort. It was pointed out, by men from phone and power companies, that line clearing was as essential as building tanks, bombs or planes. The electric lines distributed the vital power that was needed to run the machinery used to produce war material. It was also necessary to keep telephone lines clear, so that fast communications could be maintained with the far flung industrial complex of the United States.

It wasn't long before two-thirds of the Davey field force was engaged in line clearing. But it was a sadly depleted work force, key men, like experienced crew members and foremen were leaving to join some part of the war effort. Even "Red" Jacobs, who had played an important role in Davey research had joined the SeaBees. By the end of the following year, 526 Davey men were in the service. It seemed as if every family was affected, including Martin's. Alexander M. Smith, husband of Martin's daughter, Evangeline, a member of the Naval Reserves, was called to active duty in 1941 and served aboard a cruiser in the Atlantic Fleet for nearly 5 years. Martin's son, Martin L. Jr., entered the Army in February, 1943, and served until December 1945.

Some years later, in commenting on the manpower situation during the war, Frans F. Lofgren, Vice President in Charge of Sales, said, "We operated the Company during those years with old men and very young men, the rest were in service or in war industries." However, he neglected to mention, that in 1944, two young women joined the staff of Davey Tree Surgeons. They had taken a two year college course in horticulture and, according to reports at the time, they were very professional and competent.

Every effort was made by the Company to keep in touch with the men in service and with their families. Many letters were written to the men by Martin. Addresses of those in service were published in the Davey Bulletin to encourage employees to write to the men who were away serving their country. The Company's concern for the men evoked a great deal of favorable comment from their families. Typical of the letters received is this one, which appeared in the Davey Bulletin. It was in response to a letter from Martin to the parents of one of the men in service, inquiring when the son would be returning to civilian life.

> "Let me take this occasion to express our appreciation of the way you have so thoughtfully made plans for your boys and the way which you have kept in touch with their parents through these years when the boys have been away from us. It does one good to hear of companies such as yours who handle their employees as human beings, rather than cogs in a great machine. We have been most favorably impressed by the little touches you have shown and naturally our feelings towards your company are most favorable indeed."

There were also reports from men, stationed in all parts of the world, trying to gather together other Davey men for a reunion.

One of the direct results of the manpower shortage was the reduction of the sales force, from sixty-five to twenty. This meant that many sales territories were closed down for the duration of the war.

In addition to manpower and material shortages the Company had to contend with rationing of essential materials such as gasoline and tires. These conditions quickly reflected themselves in reduced volume. Once more management found it necessary to "cut the cloth to fit the suit," in other words, reduce expenses. In cooperation with this effort, the Board of Directors voted that the President be empowered to form an executive committee of three to seven men, which would have the authority to act for the full Board. Through this action they planned to reduce the number of its meetings. This in turn would effect savings on transportation and other expenses incidental to Board meetings. In other action the management was doing everything possible to balance its costs with a field force of 350 men.

While many of these events were taking place, Martin was making an important personal contribution to support the War effort. Although he had barely recovered from the severe illness he had suffered in 1941 he agreed to accept the responsibility of leading the first War Bond drive for the Kent area. The overwhelming success of the first effort, led to his being named chairman of the five succeeding bond drives. Under his thorough and untiring direction, the Kent area oversubscribed its quota in every drive. He accepted this responsibility over the protests of his doctor.

134

The whole Company was behind Martin's efforts to sell War Bonds. In February of 1944 the records show that the Davey Tree Expert Company bought $50,000 worth of bonds, Kent office personnel $20,450, Field personnel $8,975 and payroll deductions from the first of the year were $9,775 making a two month total of $89,200 that went to back the Government's action to finance the war.

In 1944 the Company responded in another way to support the war effort. The Government put out a cry for 25,000 civilians to plant gardens. To support this program, the Company published a booklet "Vegetable Garden Guide" and supplied copies free of charge. They were distributed through the foremen.

In spite of the handicaps under which it was operating, the Davey Tree Expert Company was making some positive moves to add basic strength to its future operations. Toward this end, in December of 1942, the Directors voted to buy the remaining assets of the former City Bank of Kent for $29,800. The original City Bank of Kent remained closed after the bank holiday of the Thirties. Shortly after that, it was reorganized and resumed operations under the same name.

A similar move was made in 1944. The Directors agreed to buy 5,000 acres of forest land, much of it in virgin timber, from Jim Davey. It was located in the area known as Soco Gap, which is forty miles west of Asheville, North Carolina. Jim had built a home there and had been conducting a lumbering operation. In 1943, he had suffered a heart attack and his doctors advised him to retire. The Company paid $92,000 for the land and $65,000 for the buildings. The Directors saw this as an opportunity to diversify the Company's operations.

In 1943 the Navy honored the memory of John Davey by giving one of its Liberty ships his name. The Company greatly appreciated this recognition. The bronze plaque commemorating the occasion, is prominently displayed, to this very day, in the lobby of the Company's main office.

As the war ground on, the Company continued to be plagued by manpower shortages—a situation that had a restrictive influence on its affairs. However, the shortages of people did have one meritorious effect. It had been the custom for home office personnel to perform a myriad of services for the field force. Because of the shortage of office help, these favors had to be discontinued. But more importantly, it became necessary to streamline many of the office procedures.

In a Board meeting held on February 22, 1944, Martin urged the Board of Directors, to plan a post war program for the Company. He sug-

135

gested that such a plan should have two phases; the first to be made effective at the close of the European war; the second to become operational at the end of the war in the Pacific. The subject of post-war planning was an important item on the agenda of Board meetings in the months ahead.

As a result of these meetings, it was agreed that at the end of the European war, the Company would resume a regular training program; re-establish the technical institute; prepare an advertising campaign and have it ready to release when Germany surrendered; hire and train salesmen; and finally to give prizes to employees for offering ways and methods to improve the services of the Company.

These discussions of future planning were not confined to the cloistered precincts of the Board room. Martin discussed these ideas openly with the employees and wrote about them in editorials which appeared in the Davey Bulletin. Since the men in the armed services were receiving the Bulletin, there is no doubt that these statements were important to their morale, revealing that the Company was making plans which would benefit their future.

Martin's editorials in the Davey Bulletin often dealing with post-war planning, provided some insight into his character and basic beliefs. He was religious, patriotic and believed, with a passion, in free enterprise and hard work. The following paragraphs have been excerpted from one of his editorials. They are offered here because strict adherence to the principles stated in it, made at least one man and one company successful. This is what he had to say:

"Only five things that I now think of have brought about the advancement of the human race. First, is the Christian religion, with its civilizing influence. Second, is intelligent self-interest. Third, is the capacity and willingness to deal honorably. Fourth is ambition and the creative genius it inspires. Fifth, and above everything else, is a willingness to work.

"No wealth was ever created without work. No new lands were ever explored, no new wealth discovered, without work. None of the necessities or luxuries was ever created without work. We may set it down as the inexorable law of nature that the future of the world and our country will follow the pattern of the past.

"My good old father left his native England and came to America. Millions of other sturdy sons of Europe did the same thing and for the same reasons. They were coming to the land of opportunity. America gave them not only opportunity, but gave them unprecedented personal liberties. If the United States government will give us back our liberties, and let the ambitious genius and industry of the American people have a full chance once more, and content itself with necessary regulation for the protection of the general public, we will see a new era of progress and prosperity in this greatest land on earth."

Post war planning continued to take a large part of management's time. During the first half of 1945 it was suggested that a refresher course in tree surgery techniques should be prepared to be ready to offer returning veterans. The proposers of this idea pointed out that many of the men had been in service for a long period, some of them for five years, and for this reason their skills as tree men might be rusty.

As pointed out earlier, one of the objectives of the post war plan was to hire enough salesmen to staff the forty territories that had to be abandoned during the war years. Management realized the difficulty of this task. They knew that many of the sales group would be new men with no experience in tree surgery, or knowledge of the Davey Tree Expert Company. It was proposed that a way to compensate for this lack of technical knowledge would be to team a new sales representative with an experienced field man.

In all of the planning sessions there was one common thread which Martin attempted to weave through all of the discussions. He was convinced that, in spite of the difficulties the Company had been through, opportunity would again exist for its growth and expansion. He spoke and wrote about this to the Directors and employees with an almost evangelistic fervor. He was convinced that the territories abandoned during the war could and would again be made productive. He readily pointed out that there would be changes; new people would be in the areas and in many cases property would have changed hands, but the combination would provide a bountiful supply of new prospects for the services of the Davey Tree Expert Company.

Finally, the time to put the plans into action arrived. Germany surrendered on May 7, 1945. Soon after the end of the war in Europe, the United States dropped the atomic bomb on Hiroshima and Nagasaki, forcing the unconditional surrender of Japan on August 14, 1945.

Shortly after these important events, Martin returned from a sales conference, held for men in the New York area at the Biltmore Hotel. In reporting to the Directors on this meeting, Martin made it clear that he was more convinced than ever about the need for a refresher course for returning veterans. The reason for holding the meeting in New York was that the former practice of the annual sales meetings which were held in Kent had long been abandoned. They had become another victim of first the depression, then the war. There was another reason for discontinuing the former type of annual meeting which had meant so much to the Company in the past. During the days when the Davey Institute of Tree Surgery was in full swing, it was a natural event to call in the salesmen and foremen at the end of the school term, which also marked the start of the big season in the North.

As the gigantic war machine began to be disassembled, men started to return to the Company as they were discharged from service. Seventy-nine had returned by November of 1945. By March of 1946, 189 had returned to resume their careers with Davey. Among the men returning was Martin L. Davey, Jr., who rejoined the Company shortly after his discharge from the army in December of 1945, after nearly three years of service.

Martin had been looking forward to his son's return. He planned to turn over to him the responsibilities of the Company which had been his for all these many years.

Succession must have been a subject on the minds of Martin and his Board members as indicated by an action they took on February 5th, 1946. They voted that, in the event of the death or physical incapacity of Martin, the affairs of the Company were to be placed in the hands of an operating committee, to consist of Martin L. Davey, Jr., Alexander M. Smith, son-in-law, and J. Harlan Carson, nephew. At the time it seemed like no more than a prudent safeguard.

Unfortunately, this motion had to be put into effect in less than two months. On March 31st, 1946, Martin L. Davey suffered a fatal heart attack after a pleasant evening with friends at his home in Kent. The evening had been spent playing bridge.

The death of Martin L. Davey marked the passing of a very remarkable man. He took over a debt-ridden business, that was little more than an idea and a book, and turned it into a successful enterprise of national and international fame. His business acumen served him well in other business ventures. He had a brilliant and successful political career as a mayor, congressman and governor. He was mourned by people in all walks of life.

A poem, by Henry Van Dyke, used to close his funeral service, seems to sum up his life:

So let the way wind up the hill or down,
O'er rough or smooth, the journey will be joy:
Still seeking what I sought but when a boy
New friendships, high adventure and a crown,
My heart will keep the courage of the quest
And hope the road's last turn will be the best.

Now, the leadership of the Davey Tree Expert Company would pass to younger hands.

XVIII   A New Generation Takes Over

It was quite clear that Martin wanted his son to succeed him as President of the Davey Tree Expert Company. He had planned for a period of training which would have included a gradual turnover of the responsibilities of running the Company.

Fate, as we now know, intervened and prevented the orderly transition from father to son. Martin L. Davey, Jr., was twenty-eight years old when his father died and he became President of the Davey Tree Expert Company. It was a difficult period in his life. He had only been back from the army for less than four months, during which time, he had to pick up the threads of his marriage and his career that had been interrupted by nearly three years in the army. He also had to get acquainted with his son, who had been born while he was in the service and was twenty-two months old when he first met him. Added to the difficulties of re-adjusting to civilian life, was the shock and grief of his father's death.

During the few months after Martin L. Davey, Jr., returned to the Company, it appeared that his father was putting a great deal of pressure on him. Night after night, Martin insisted that his son join him after dinner, to discuss the business.

There were almost endless hours discussing key people in the organization; their strengths, their weaknesses, their potential. Many of those under discussion, would have been surprised and amazed at how well the "boss" knew them. It seemed as though Martin had a premonition that time was running out . . . that he had to use every precious moment to educate and train his son for the responsibility of heading the Company.

It was on April 3, 1946, that Martin L. Davey, Jr., was elected President, Treasurer and General Manager of the Davey Tree Expert Company. Other officers elected at the same time were: Paul H. Davey, Executive Vice-President; Charles L. May, Second Vice-President; Alexander M. Smith, Third Vice-President; and Hugo Birkner, Fourth Vice-President.

Martin L. Davey, Jr., has been known throughout most of his life as "Brub," a nickname that came about when, as small children, the younger of his two sisters pronounced the word brother as "Brubbo." The family quickly adopted the term and the name used affectionately by the family, became permanent and Martin L. Davey, Jr., became known and remains Brub to all of his associates inside and outside of the Company.

Brub Davey brought to his new position, both academic and practical training. A graduate of Yale University, his major was Botany with a minor in Business Administration. His practical experience came about from working as a tree surgeon in the Chicago territory during his summer vacation from college in 1938. After graduation, in June of 1940, he did personnel work for the Company until he left for the army in February of 1943.

He had one other tool to guide him in his somewhat awesome responsibilities . . . a letter written to him by his father, which he received shortly after his return from the army. The letter was a summary of Martin L. Davey's business philosophy. While it was helpful to Brub, it also provides some insight into Martin's success.

> Kent, Ohio
> December 19, 1945.

My Son,

Now that you have returned from Army service, it is my desire that you take over the active management of The Davey Tree Expert Company, with whatever help and advice you need from me. Ever since my severe heart attack nearly five years ago, my health and strength have been gradually declining. The strain of the war years has not helped.

This is a good and honorable business. It is in sound condition, has excellent personnel, and enjoys a fine reputation. It has been a hundred years in the making—John Davey was born a century ago. To the building of this business I have given forty years of my own life. It has not been easy to bring it through all the trials and vicissitudes of that long and rapidly changing period.

You will be the third generation to carry our business and professional banner. I hope your most zealous ambition will be to carry it forward unsullied. I hope, also, that you will take to heart the following advice, because, my Son, there is no sub-stitute for experience.

As I ponder the question, what things to put first, it seems that there are several of equal importance. And so, I will set them down as they occur to me, in what, you might say, is a summary of my business philosophy.

Above everything, make your word good. But, and this is terribly important, be very careful about the promises you make. Take time to get the facts, weigh each matter carefully on its merits, then when you make a commitment, keep your word under all possible circumstances and at whatever cost. If you ever find that it is impossible to keep a promise, for perfectly valid reasons or because of things beyond your control, then—don't de-lay—tell the other person promptly and frankly.

Next, I would say, is to think of your clients before every-thing else. They are your life blood. Make it your business to see that they get honest value, quality workmanship and diligent, conscientious service. They will continue to pay a fair price for that kind of service, sufficient to yield a moderate profit with proper management.

Nearly all of our clients are good people. Therefore, if one of them makes a complaint, see that it is promptly and fairly investigated, for the purpose of equitable adjustment. You should assume that the client believes he is right, and let him know by our conduct that we mean to be right. It is very rare that one of our clients has ever tried to chisel or defraud us. In such unusual cases, make him pay, and never serve him again. The kind of peo-ple for whom we work, who love their trees, are nearly always persons of fine and superior character.

How can you give such good service? Just don't try to run a reform school. You can't make good men out of poor ones. I tried it many years ago, and it simply will not work. If a man is lazy, let him go. If he is careless and indifferent, let him go. If he is dishonest, let him go. It follows, quite naturally, that you have left only men who are diligent, careful, interested and honest. There are sufficient good men available for an interesting and honorable work like ours. Therefore, if you weed out the poor ones as fast as they are found, you will always have good ones to serve our clients.

Treat your employees as human beings. Good men are am-bitious, frugal and trustworthy. Therefore, you should reward the better men as they earn it, when and as they prove themselves, and before they have to ask for it. Be on your guard against the men who recommend themselves too loudly and aggressively. I have found that some of the best men are a little too modest to push themselves forward. It is part of your job to find that kind and reward them voluntarily.

I have always felt that good sales representatives should make good money, and have always been happy to see them do so. Make sure, however, that they sell and deliver the kind and quality of Davey service that represents true Davey standards, principles and ethics. I do not quite agree with Emerson when he said, "If a man makes a better mouse-trap, the world will make a beaten path to his door." That might be true in a small community, but not in a great country like America. You can't get anywhere with a sizable business without good salesmen. No matter how good the thing is which you produce, you must sell it or go out of business. It goes without saying that the thing which the salesman sells must be really good or he is soon out of employment.

Watch your credit with a jealous eye, every phase of it. Don't ever let a note become overdue, unless there is no way to prevent it. Pay your notes on time. Pay your bills promptly. Take all cash discounts. Make it one of the first orders of your business life to protect your credit, pay your bills, and have money in the bank to meet payrolls and all other proper and necessary business expenses.

This brings me to the next thing of great and equal importance. Watch expenses like a hawk. Question every expense that is not clearly necessary and wise. Bore into these things with determination and relentless purpose. Never hesitate to order an unnecessary expense eliminated and see that it is done. Any money that is wasted must come out of the clients or the employees or the stockholders. Many people will suggest ideas to spend money —other people's money. Most of them are bad. Occasionally you will get a good one. Put every such suggestion to the acid test, "Is it a good and necessary thing for the business?" One of your most important jobs is to say "No," and make it stick.

On the matter of expenses, I have had a rule in effect for the last several years that no one could incur any new expense or increase any present expense without my definite prior approval. Experience has made this rule necessary; results have proved it wise. Some folks love to give orders and spend money—especially other people's money. Some other folks like to make themselves popular by readily agreeing to ideas of spending or by favoring those who try to chisel. In self-defense and for the protection of the future interests of the Company and all its employees, you must continue the above mentioned rule, or your regrets will be many and severe.

There is an old saying, "When in doubt do nothing." There is some merit in it. Many a time I have waited to think things over, get more facts, and weigh the arguments pro and con, and by so doing have avoided some bad decisions. Earlier in life I was guilty of making some snap judgments that were rather costly. Please understand that a necessary part of your daily work will be to make decisions, and I am not advising you to put them off. Quite the contrary, you must make decisions every day and get things done—you understand, get things done even if you make a few mistakes. But don't make snap judgments.

You must make a reasonable profit, if you expect to stay in business. There is no Santa Claus for private business. When your profits disappear, you are on the way out. Therefore, it is part of your job to know your costs, all your costs, and all your sources of revenue, and whether your revenues are adequate to cover all your necessary and proper costs and leave a fair profit. If and when you have made a reasonably good profit, and when you have the money in the bank, you can afford to be a little extra generous with the employees who helped you make it.

I would advise and urge that you stay out of the banking business; that is, lending money to employees, unless it is unavoidable. There always have been and always will be many such requests. It is quite natural. Usually, it is neither wise nor necessary. If a man is of the right sort, he can get credit elsewhere and should do so.

My reason? You must protect and husband your working capital. Suppose a hundred men each would ask for a loan of a thousand dollars to buy trucks or cars or homes. That would be a hundred thousand dollars. Two hundred fifty. such loans would be a quarter of a million, and then you might find it difficult to meet payrolls and your current bills.

Furthermore, whenever you lend money, you create more bookkeeping, and it takes time of home-office people that should be used on regular Company business. The average person would be amazed if he knew the enormous amount of time required of the Accounting Department by Uncle Sam's innumerable laws, rules and regulations—payroll deductions, bookkeeping, records, remittances and reports, ad infinitum, plus the multitudinous bookkeeping records and reports required by all the states. Actually, I would almost dread the ordeal of starting a new business today. Unless you could afford to hire competent outsiders, you would have to be a manysided lawyer, an expert accountant with varied knowledge and experience, a financial expert, an operating genius, a public relations expert, a labor-relations expert, a diplomat and a diplomatic driver, a leader who is willing to take a clubbing by various and sundry little tyrants representing the government or others; and you would have to have the patience of Job, the perseverance of Columbus, and the stamina of Atlas.

Now for a few other things. Never do anything while you are angry. It probably will be wrong. If you feel highly incensed by something, write it down on paper and thus get it out of your system—but put the paper in your desk or in your pocket for a few days, and then you will probably feel differently and do differently. I have made some mistakes by not doing this.

Pay a man everything that is coming to him. If he adds up his expenses incorrectly, it is your duty to make it right and pay him in full. But if he puts in more than he has coming, don't pay the excess. If he is honest, he will be glad to be corrected. If he is trying to chisel, he knows he doesn't have it coming. Likewise, if a client pays more than his bill, send him the difference. If he pays his bill twice, send his second check back promptly with a polite explanation. (You would be surprised to know how many have paid twice.)

Don't do something merely because a competitor does it, or merely because some well-meaning friend or associate thinks it is a good idea. Of course, you should never be against it for that reason. It might or might not be a good thing. Judge everything strictly on its merit—calmly, judicially and deliberately.

Please, please, do not try to be popular in your business dealings. You simply can't manage a business properly and be popular with everyone. Some people are inclined to slow down and take it easy; they need to be spurred into action. Some are inclined to chisel if they can get away with it, they need sharp discipline. Some few may become cocky or overbearing or impolite; they need to have their wings clipped and to be brought back to earth.

However, you should try to deserve respect. To achieve this desirable end, you should always be just and fair and reasonably tolerant of minor human frailties. In the long run, the solid qualities of character and the old fashioned virtues are of far greater importance than brilliance or shrewdness . . .

Beware of flatterers. They have a cunning way of wasting your valuable time, or trying to get something they are not entitled to. When anyone attempts to flatter you or give you profuse compliments, put a big question mark after everything he says or does. Preferably, don't deal with him.

Save your own time, and see that all others respect your time. It is extremely valuable. Parcel it out systematically among people and things according to the order of their importance to the business. Some people talk too much and others are a bit shy. It is easy to tell the difference. Just take time enough to get all the essentials and then make your decision, or say you will think it over (preferably the latter) and end the interview, going promptly to the next most important thing.

Speaking of time and the necessity of conserving it, you should not burden yourself with details. You must employ others for that. Know all you can about every phase of the business, but get your information from reliable people who handle the details. No man can manage a business wisely or efficiently unless he gets his head up off his desk part of the time and does some intensive and constructive thinking.

If you expect others to be diligent workers, you must be one yourself. Set an example of diligence. Running an organization is serious business. It is not a social affair nor a fraternity tete-a-tete. One of the most successful men I knew years ago said to me, "For every business that succeeds, someone must give his life."

You ought to be friendly in a moderate and reserved sort of way—I mean genuinely friendly. And always be polite to everyone. When you give orders, always say, "please." It costs nothing and makes the order easy to take. For many years, whenever I have sent orders by wire, I have always used the word "please" even if it were necessary to pay for an extra word. Everyone with any sense will know it is an order just the same. The occasional dumbbell who thinks he can disobey because you say "please," or who thinks you are soft for that reason, should be taken off the payroll promptly. Polite firmness pays dividends.

There is one thing about business that is crystal clear. You can never coast down hill. There never comes a time when you can sit back, blandly and comfortably and feel that your work is done, that all your problems are solved for a considerable period into the future. Problems continue to arise, some small and some large. There will likely be fewer serious problems, however, if you are diligent, watchful and active every day. A successful business is like a well-made and well-oiled vehicle that travels steadily up-grade, always and forever up-grade.

We live and move and have our being in a selfish world. But that is not all bad. It is self-interest that makes the world move forward. Intelligent and properly harnessed selfishness is good for mankind. It is grasping, unfair, cheating selfishness that is a curse. All good business is founded on intelligent self-interest, that of the customer and the employee and the company. Those interests must all be served, if a concern is to last beyond a brief time. Those interests are mutual in many respects, and they should never be in serious conflict with each other. You must give and get full value.

In all my experience in business and in public life, the rarest types of minds I have encountered are the judicial and the creative. Most of us are the victims of what we have been told is true. We accept what we have learned and go blithely on our way. That is probably the reason why there are so few original or creative thinkers. John Davey is a good example of the rare exception. During all the prior history of intelligent mankind, it had always been assumed that nothing could be done to save trees by surgical methods. His original thinking and creative action gave the world a new science and a new profession.

But the judicial mind, how rare that is! So many of us are the victims of our likes and dislikes, our prejudices, our preconceived notions, and our own peculiar idiosyncrasies. If someone whom we dislike suggests something, we are against it. The judicial mind discards its own likes and dislikes, and judges everything on the basis of pure facts and proven merit. Therefore, I would urge you strongly to strive always to be judicial in your thinking about all things.

It is well to work earnestly toward perfection. You will never reach it, of course, in this imperfect world, but if you keep striving for it manfully and persistently your business will be infinitely better than it could possibly be otherwise. In fact, I sincerely believe that if you do not continuously work and strive toward perfection, your business will steadily go down-hill toward a deserved oblivion. The natural pull of human inertia and indifference is downward. Good management must pull steadily the other way, and pull harder than the normal laws of human nature.

And last, but not least, never be conceited or vain or pompous or too self-important. I am sure you are not that way by nature, but I wanted to give this special word of caution. If a man is conceited or too opinionated, he cannot think straight or act wisely. Never let success spoil you. I do not think it would, but these thoughts are a very ardent part of my philosophy. Keep yourself reasonably humble but self-reliant. Keep yourself natural and unspoiled. When difficulties or discouragements confront you, summon all your calm, determined moral courage and keep going —forward.

While the letter covers many specific details, it also seems a reflection of another piece of philosophy which has continued to be helpful in guiding the fortunes of the Davey Tree Expert Company: "Do it right or not at all."

XIX Keep Going Forward

The last three words in Martin's letter to his son, "keep going forward" almost seemed to become a battle cry. The Davey Tree Expert Company started to move forward under Brub Davey's leadership. The sales volume for 1946 reached a new high of $3,943,000 which was $800,000 more than the total for 1929, the best previous year in the Company's history.

This initial success was not brought about without some struggle. Change, even when it's minor, or whatever the cause, always seems to meet a degree of resistance. So it was when the major change of leadership occurred in the Davey Tree Expert Company. There were those who questioned whether a man of Brub's age and experience could run the Company successfully. Some of these seriously considered leaving the Company to strike out on their own. But Brub, along with some of the older and cooler heads, led by Dallas Marria, the top utility salesman persuaded the would-be defectors to stay with the Company, and at least give Brub an opportunity to prove himself. He did prove himself a capable leader and in the years ahead, he took the Company to heights that would have seemed astronomical to his father and his grandfather.

Holding the organization together was a major victory. It enabled Brub and his management team to press forward in several directions. The Davey Institute of Tree Surgery was reopened but with a difference from the earlier schools. The school term was reduced from three months to six weeks. This was accomplished by limiting the course of study to tree surgery. In the former curriculum a number of academic subjects were taught. Also, in the past, there had been an extensive extracurricular athletic program offered. This too was eliminated in the interest of saving time to permit covering all the essentials of tree surgery. One of the principal reasons for the shorter periods of instruction was that the increased volume from utilities resulted in plenty of work during the winter, so there was no longer a need to provide an activity to hold good men on the payroll over the winter, formerly an off season.

The school opened under this new plan during the winter of 1946-47. The first class consisted of 30 students, most of them veterans of the war, several had been officers. Another class was brought in for instruction during that winter. Red Jacobs, who had been placed at the head of the Institute, remarked years later that he remembered these men as being of exceptionally high caliber.

The kind of men represented in this class is illustrated in a story told about Herb Winters, who was one of the men attending the first post-war institute. It seems that he, and a group of other Davey students, were visiting one of the local watering spas, when a slightly inebriated gentleman walked into the bar, waving a pistol. Herb, ordinarily a very quiet person, had been a Ranger during the War, didn't like the pistol waving. He politely offered the man a choice; put the gun away or be forced to eat it. The drunk persisted. Hardly before anyone realized that was happening, Herb moved in, and using Ranger tactics, disarmed the man. While Herb didn't make the man eat the gun, he did make everyone in the place feel a lot safer and much more comfortable. While there was no requirement that Davey Tree Surgeons had to go around disarming drunks, the job did call for men with courage and a taste for adventure. Certainly, Herb Winters, and his associates, had an appetite for both.

While some of the old timers, who had attended the earlier schools when the term was three months long, may have thought that the new men were having an easy time of it because they had to attend for only six weeks, quite the contrary was true. In order to cover all of the essential material, it was necessary to put in long days and many night sessions as well.

The faculty of the institute was made up of Davey Tree Surgeons and men from the research staff of the Company. In addition to these people, outside authorities were brought in to lecture on specialized areas of the tree business. An example of this type of program was a film presentation made by a representative of the telephone company who was a safety engineer and a teacher of first aid.

The film dealt with the laying of the co-axial cable, which ran cross country to connect several large cities and played an important role in telephone and TV service. Of special interest to the students was the part

Davey played in the project, which consisted of preparing fence openings, cutting down trees in the right of way, and the complete removal of stumps and rocks that would interfere with the laying of the cable.

Two other very important steps were taken during 1946 which were of special interest to the employees of the Davey Tree Expert Company. One was the announcement that the Company was going to put into effect a profit sharing plan. It provided that forty percent of the profits before taxes would be set aside and divided among the employees according to an established formula. The other employee benefit was the announcement of an improvement in the group insurance plan which would, as a result, provide greater benefits.

Also during 1946, Brub decided to revive an old tradition, the annual sales meetings held in Kent. Plans were made and the first sales convention in many years was held in January of 1947, at the Twin Lakes Country Club, located just outside of Kent. It was attended by seventy-five men, whose total combined experience in the tree business was 1,350 years.

Brub had good news to present to the convention. The profit sharing for 1946 was greater than had been forecast, because the year turned out to be the greatest in the Company's history.

As if all of these things were not enough, Brub and his management were planning the introduction of a new service, chemical brush control. The idea was conceived by Red Jacobs in 1946 and brought into being in 1947. Red had returned from the SeaBees in 1945 with the idea that chemical brush control had the potential of being a profitable service, if Davey could sell the idea to the public utilities. Up to that time, the phone and power companies employed crews of men to remove brush by hand. Following World War II it was almost impossible to find men willing to do this kind of hard work.

Red was aware that DuPont was developing a chemical called Ammate. He had also been following the experiments being conducted with 2-4D. However, no one was quite sure how effective these new chemicals would be in brush control. Always seeking demonstrable proof for any new idea, Red, in 1946, tried spraying a few experimental plots in Ohio, Arkansas and Pennsylvania. Checking, the following Spring, he found a lot of dead brush. He also concluded that Ammate was the most effective chemical for this purpose.

The Davey Tree Expert Company then decided to offer its utility customers this new service . . . chemical brush control. The first assignment came from the telephone company in Arkansas. From there the idea

151

*DAVEY TREE EXPERT CO. SALES CONVENTION
AT TWIN LAKES COUNTRY CLUB*
January, 1947

First Row:
W. R. "Shorty" Williams
George White
Charles W. "Shorty" Frederick
Frank Lancaster
Lou Irvine
Urb Throm
Cliff Bissler
Bill Bailey
Martin Davey, Jr.
D. Q. "Red" Grove
Hugo Birkner
Charlie May
Gail Chenoweth
Dallas Marria
E. P. Metcalf

Second Row:
Ross McCafferty
Paul Hershey
?
Ty Cobb
Mitch Foster
Jack Riddle
L. V. Newton
Don Fowler
?
Bill Lauck
Al Landberg
Jack Allen
Jack Bouvy
?
Luke Swanger
Milton Hooper

Third Row:
Joe Heston
Herb Rice
Bob Sands
Ed Bowen
O. B. Crosser
Dan Hayman
Norton McDermott
Jim Buckman
Jack McNees
Billy White
Bill Parker
Decker Magruder
Gus Lehman
Barton Smith
Vernon Hill
Ben Britton

Back Row:
Will Havnes
George Bassler
E. I. Kabel
Ray Landis
Herb Knowles
Bob Sours
Howard Spellacy
Corliss Hoge
Frans "Red" Lofgren
Jerry Landis
Perry Hudson
Charlie Toner
Wally Emerson
Murray Swanson

*Chemical brush control right-of-way
spraying in the late 1940s.*

quickly spread to others. The first year the service was offered, it produced a $50,000 volume; it jumped to $250,000 the next year. Within a few years the annual volume for chemical brush control reached a million dollars.

In offering this new service, Davey caught its competition flat-footed. Many of them learned about the new chemicals from the salesmen of the chemical companies. As they rushed in to compete they made serious mistakes. Only the Davey Tree Expert Company was able to offer a service backed by sound research. Davey has remained a leader in brush control service.

During World War II, the introduction of a new tool, the power chain saw, was to have a far reaching effect on the profession of tree surgery. The first of these power chain saws, was introduced in the Chicago territory. The saws were manufactured by the Mall Company. The idea of the cutting chain came from saws captured from the German Army. Although the first saws were made in a limited number and rationed dur-

153

ing the war, Davey was permitted to buy two of them for use in utility work which had been declared essential to the war effort. Those first saws were far from perfected. They were big, ponderous affairs, requiring two men to operate them. They were used principally for tree removal. E. P. Metcalfe recalled that he was continually hauling a saw back to the Mall Company for repairs. Davey men helped to solve some of the mechanical problems encountered in the use of these early models. Metcalfe also reported that he carried a large supply of parts in his car, so that repairs and replacements could be made in the field. Even though these first power saws needed a great deal of attention, they proved to be a useful tool. It wasn't long after the initial purchase, that a third saw was added.

The next manufacturer of power chain saws was the Disston Saw Company. However, they were so heavy the men didn't like them. But as time moved on, power saws were improved in every way. They became lighter and more dependable, making them an essential tool for the tree surgery crews. The use of power saws spread rapidly. In fact by 1957, foremen owned 430 of them which they leased to the Davey Tree Company on an hourly basis. Paul Hershey pointed out that, "Today, a power

The latest in two man power saw.

saw can remove a tree in minutes that in the 'good old days,' took many gruelling hours."

But even though exciting new things were happening to the Tree Company, there were still worrisome details that had to be faced. One of the larger problems was the state of the equipment following the war. Almost everyone, including the foremen, were driving old cars, many of them with recapped tires. The Company's trucks and trailers, in spite of a careful maintenance program, were a sorry collection and were in various stages of decay. Some of the more urgent needs were discussed in a Board Meeting held in December of 1947. It was pointed out, at that time, the Company had to purchase during the next year; five Dodge Power wagons for $11,000; a Cletrac Tractor for $30,000; twenty power sprayers for $32,000. In addition, although no dollar amount was mentioned, it was also agreed that a number of standard trucks were needed. On top of all this, $50,000 was required for an inventory of Ammate.

Other problems were discussed at the same meeting, both requiring fairly substantial investments. One of the subjects that kept coming up before the Board was that of owning or renting warehouse space. The Company, by now, had a number of warehouses scattered across the country and in Canada. The rental charges were becoming a sizeable item of expense. Because of that, it was only natural that the subject of whether it was better to own or rent would come up from time to time. Eventually a program was developed to own the majority of the sites. Toward this end, the Board, at its December 1947 meeting, voted to appropriate $18,500 for land for a warehouse in Greenwich, Connecticut.

The Board was informed during that same session, that $17,500 was needed to purchase eight mist blowers. They were required to tool-up for a new service to be launched in 1948.

As 1947 drew to a close another substantial gain was recorded. Sales during Brub's first full year as President of the Company were $4,609,000. This was a gain of nearly $700,000 over the previous year.

The combination of increased volume and the requirement for equipment, resulted in the need for more cash to run the business. Consequently, the estimate of borrowing from banks, made earlier in the year, was exceeded by $50,000.

In order to ease some of the pressure for money, the Company sold part of its Soco Gap, North Carolina, land to the Carolina Wood Turning Company for $37,500. Part of the proceeds from this sale went to finance the warehouse and shop at Greenwich, Connecticut. It was also reported that the Company might be forced to sell to the state of North Carolina

1,200 to 1,400 acres of the North Carolina property to be used for the Blue Ridge Parkway. This would take most of Soco Gap and would confiscate the buildings built by Jim Davey. Also, it would include a roadway which had been built through Bear Pen Gap. All of this property was eventually sold and at a substantial profit to the Company.

At the end of 1947, Brub had been President of the Davey Tree Expert Company for twenty-one months. During that relatively short period a great deal had been accomplished. Employee benefits had been improved, the institute had been reopened, sales volume had been increased substantially, the annual sales convention had been revived, and a new profitable service had been launched. He was following his father's admonition to . . . keep going forward.

XX Volume Up— Profits Down

As the Davey Tree Expert Company moved into 1948, the management was filled with optimism. The Company had just completed two record-breaking years and the forecast for 1948 indicated further growth.

As Brub looked back over the year just completed, it was with a certain sense of satisfaction because many problems had been met and solved. One of these was the difficulty of finding cars and trucks, both for the Company and for the men returning from the armed services.

W. R. "Shorty" Williams, a Director, was given the assignment by the Board of solving the problem. As men returned to the Company from the armed services, their experience was badly needed in the field. But, before they could become fully operative they needed cars for transportation. And since some of them were foremen, they needed trucks. Williams had established a good rapport with the car and truck manufacturers so he was able to get what the men needed. He was successful in replacing almost every piece of motorized equipment owned by the Davey Tree Expert Company.

If there was a euphoric feeling, it is easy to understand; that it was short lived, is equally easy to comprehend, because when a company goes through a period of rapid growth, there are always problems that need management's attention. So it was with Davey. The difficulties they faced were of a positive nature and stemmed from the increased demand for its services. One of the problems which seemed to be everlasting was finding enough men to staff the field force, another was to find housing for the squad members.

Each of these areas was worked on and solutions were found. In the case of housing for the men, the foremen worked on that and solved it. It was time consuming, often requiring going up and down the streets of a town looking for suitable quarters to house the squads. In the recruitment area they drew heavily on the past experiences and there were at least three new items in the recruitment kit. These were: the Institute which had been reopened during the post-war period which made it possible to offer candidates positions with professional training and the profit sharing plan was changed, so a person had only to be on the payroll for six months, instead of five years, before becoming a participant, a change that was a real advantage in hiring people. A movie had been produced titled, "Your Future in the Trees." The central character was Henry Schmid. The film related his experiences in being hired and trained by the Davey Tree Expert Company. Schmid later became advertising manager of the Company.

When a company experiences a period of prosperity such as the one Davey was going through, there is a tendency to loosen up the purse strings and spend more freely than is the usual practice. So it was not strange that in reviewing the Company's fiscal performance in May of 1948, the Directors were faced with some figures which seemed to call for corrective action. While they were encouraged by the fact that sales were up seventeen percent they were concerned because direct costs were up sixteen percent; sales costs were up ten percent and management expenses were up twenty percent. While some expenses were down, like advertising and general expenses, they were not able to offset the costs which had increased. Also the Company had borrowed $150,000 from the banks.

This examination of the figures led management to adopt a more conservative program for the balance of the year. As a result of this decision, the various line items on the financial statement showed a satisfactory improvement by the end of the year.

Even though expenses were being carefully watched, management of the Davey Tree Expert Company was pressing forward. It was during 1948 when the Company initiated another new service—Mist Blowing.

The mist blower was developed by George Daugherty, General Manager of the Speed Sprayer Company of Orlando, Florida. Red Jacobs and some of his people from the Research and Technical Center studied the equipment and recommended that Davey buy several of the units. These were large pieces of machinery that were mounted on the rear of a truck and employed a huge fan to blow the spray material out in a cloud-like mist. In this method of spraying, air was the vehicle which carried

Insect control through mist blowing in the 1950s.

the chemical to the trees or plants. In hydraulic spraying, water was used as the chemical carrier. Mist blowing was excellent for spraying rows of trees, such as those found on a tree-lined street. This new service made an important contribution to the growing sales volume of the Company.

Mist blowing called for men to be trained in the special techniques necessary for the proper use of the equipment. But the training was an inbuilt requirement for Davey Tree Surgeons. The Company had spent thousands of dollars in this direction.

While the Institute received a great deal of attention, there was another type of training which was important in its own right. Between the time a man was hired and before being assigned to a squad, he went through a three week training period. A great deal of this kind of training went on in the field because costs made it prohibitive to bring all the men into Kent. During the first years of Brub's leadership, field training facilities were increased. One of these training centers was located in Sa-

159

vannah, Georgia, on the grounds of the Bethesda Orphanage. Ross Mc-Cafferty the Employment Manager, sent Ellwood Boyles there to take charge. He was assisted by Bob Herbst, a veteran foreman from Long Island, who taught the techniques of cavity filling. Pat Scheinoha, a member of the Kent training staff, was in charge of teaching the proper methods of tree pruning. He was assisted by Carl Carpenter, Gene Hannrahan and George Wells.

In the area of training, the requirements for the candidates selected to attend the Davey Institute of Tree Surgery had become much more demanding than at any time previously. Not only was the choice of men much more selective, but they were required to complete the ten-lesson, 225-page extension course on tree surgery before they were accepted by the Institute. In fact, "Red" Jacobs, who headed the Institute at the time, was on record as stating that any man not interested in spending the necessary time to complete the extension course was not worth further training at Company expense.

While a great deal of time, effort and money went into teaching men the skills required for a successful career in tree surgery, another kind of training, safety on the job . . . went on continuously. The men were taught first-aid, they were cautioned about the dangers that the various tools and equipment presented. An example of the success of this program is offered by the statistics for 1948, which showed that 226 squads had no accidents for the year. In fact, the Company has a remarkable safety record, when it is considered that tree surgery offers numerous possibilities for accidents.

The thorough training of men was a firm expression on the part of the Davey Tree Expert Company, that they wanted their field squads to be professional in every sense of the word. This desire for professionalism even carried over to the men's dress. Foremen were urged to get their squads to dress in the Davey uniform, instead of overalls or non-descript clothing. Squads dressed in the forest green blouse and breeches with high top boots made a very impressive appearance. For the same reason, all Davey vehicles were painted a standard green with white doors and bumpers. The Davey name was prominently displayed on the doors.

Training in the field and at the Institute was constant but, by the same token, Davey had a rich source of experience within its organization. As early as 1947, there were 254 people on the payroll with service records of ten years or more. This experience was one of the Company's most valuable assets and one which never appeared on the balance sheet simply because no one has ever been able to properly put a value on a year's worth of experience.

It was during these years that Brub became concerned about the business mix of the Company. When he took over as President in 1946, only thirty percent of the volume was in tree surgery; the balance was in line clearing for utilities. The reason was due to the manpower shortage during the war years, which resulted in many of the sales territories being abandoned during that period. This, plus the fact that line clearing was essential to the war efforts resulted in every bit of available manpower being put on these important assignments.

While line clearing was good business, tree surgery was often more profitable. Brub's goal was to continue building line clearing volume. At the same time he wanted to increase other services to forty percent of the sales volume. Real progress was made towards this goal. In 1945, in the midst of the war, tree surgery represented twenty percent of the volume; in 1946, it rose to thirty percent and finally did reach forty percent. One of the ways Brub attacked the problem was to put two, or more, salesmen in a territory. One man was assigned to take care of the utility business. The others devoted their efforts to developing all of the other business in the area. At first, this decision met with some resistance from the salesmen, but it wasn't long before they recognized its wisdom.

In the face of all of the excitement of new services, a burgeoning volume and an improved service mix, profits were not satisfactory. This condition was brought about by the rising costs of almost everything concerned with carrying on the business. As a result, the Company was forced to raise its prices in 1948.

Even though the prices were increased the demand for Davey services continued to grow. At least a part of this growth was due to the favorable attention the Company was receiving in the media as a result of some excellent work on the part of Don Fowler who at the time was in charge of public relations and advertising for the Company. Some of the largest and most prestigious publications and broadcasters featured various aspects of the Company. Some of these were; *Parade,* a Sunday newspaper supplement, with five million circulation which ran a feature on tree moving and *American Home Magazine,* which reached more than two million families, carried an article on "How to Plant A Tree." The instructions were written and credited to the Davey Tree Expert Company; Galen Thrulesen, a writer for the *Saturday Evening Post,* one of the most influential magazines of that period, wrote an article, "A Day In The Life

161

Of A Davey Tree Surgeon" and Galen Drake a well known radio commentator, did a whole show on the life of John Davey. It was broadcast over the ABC radio network. Another informative article appeared in *Mill and Factory,* a business publication directed to the interests of management, production and maintenance people. The article dealt with the advantages of properly landscaping a factory to give a campus look to an industrial location. It gave a long list of locations where this had been done and in which Davey had played an important role. These assignments often called for the moving of large trees to give a new site a finished look.

Obviously all of this attention helped to enhance and further build the fine reputation the Davey Tree Expert Company enjoyed. In addition to all of the publicity, Davey advertising continued to appear in magazines of wide circulation.

One of the peripheral benefits of all of the publicity, was that it helped to build a strong sense of pride in the people employed by the Company. To read about one's occupation, or to hear it discussed over the air, helped to build and keep the fine spirit Davey employees exhibited over the years. Management also did its part in keeping this spirit alive, by emphasizing the important role its people played in the success of the Company. Toward this end, seven more of the Company's employees were elected to the Board of Directors in 1948. They were; Mrs. Sarah Deubner, Paul G. Hershey, Emmett Allen, Frans F. Lofgren, Homer L. Jacobs, Howard I. Spellacy and Vernon Hill.

The recognition of employees who had made an important contribution to the Company, was a reflection of the Company's belief in corporate responsibility. This attitude was amply revealed in the numerous benefit programs it provided all of its workers. It was also expressed in the Company's participation in community affairs. It was for this reason that, in 1948, the Kent Chamber of Commerce awarded the Davey Tree Expert Company its distinguished service medal for the Company's outstanding contribution, made in behalf of civic projects for the benefit of the community and its people. For a somewhat similar reason, the United States Department of State awarded Davey a plaque to express its appreciation for the financial assistance provided by the Company and its employees to support the Radio Free Europe Program.

During these postwar years while the Company was drawing some very favorable attention to itself, it was also experiencing some important changes in the way it was operating in the field. The day was fast disappearing when a few hand tools used by skilled workmen could carry on the work of the Company, the business was now using an increasing amount of mechanized equipment. Actually the move in this direction began in the Twenties when heavy equipment was used for tree moving; power spraying also came into use at that time. But then the trend was delayed, first by the Depression and then by the War. Some idea of the acceleration in this direction can be gained from the fact that from 1945 to 1949 the Company invested $482,000 in heavy equipment and $42,000

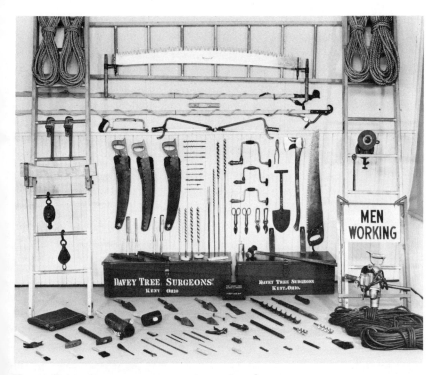

How a Davey tree surgery crew was equipped
in the 1940s and 1950s.

in mechanized equipment such as power saws. It was costing more to equip a Davey crew than ever before. The wholesale cost of the tools the Company supplied to a single three-man Davey squad was $444. Previously tools were supplied and owned by the men.

In addition to a large investment in equipment, the Company had $259,000 invested in real estate which was directly related to the operation of the business. Another area which tied up substantial amounts of capital, was the large inventory the Company was forced to carry in parts and material. In one typical year, 1949, this investment amounted to $121,000. In the Greenwich warehouse alone, the inventory included fifty-five kinds of tree surgery materials, forty different air compressor tools, twenty-two chain saw parts, two thousand sprayer parts and eighty-four parts for trucks. In addition, the warehouse in one year distributed seventy tons of seventeen different kinds of spray material.

All of this investment in real estate, equipment and inventory was the result of the tremendous growth the Company was experiencing. The capital to finance the growth, which seemed to be taking place in every part of the Davey business, came largely from earnings. Management was forced to borrow larger sums of money, this too, had to be repaid from profits. The Company was also extending a great deal more credit to its own customers. This, too, was a result of expansion and is indicated in a comparison of the accounts receivable in 1945 which were $219,000. In 1949 this figure had grown to $693,000.

In addition to all of the money the Company had invested in equipment, the foremen had a substantial investment in cars and trucks, which were used in the business. While the figure was constantly changing, it was estimated at one point in 1949 that the foremen owned 176 vehicles, some old, some new. The replacement value of these was set at $353,000.

The foremen's ownership of certain tools, cars and trucks, provoked a rather interesting discussion during a session of the "Young President's Organization." Brub, as a member of the group, was invited, as were others, to explain the operation of his company. When he related the importance of the salesmen in managing a territory, and that the foremen owned some of the equipment and managed their crews, many of those in attendance could not understand why those men didn't take off and go into business on their own.

Actually, as Brub pointed out, there was a great deal more to the business than appeared on the surface. He knew only only too well the amount of money the Company needed to invest in the hiring and training of men, the efforts that had been made to make the job good enough to combat the temptation to quit, the ability to extend credit as well as being able to borrow substantial sums of money. Another important advantage was the reputation the Davey Tree Expert Company had built up over the years, based on the philosophy of "Do it right or not at all," made it much easier to sell Davey services than those of a relatively unknown source. There were many other advantages the Company had which a small operator could not support, such as the technical and research center, sophisticated training programs and most of all, a seasoned management.

In any event, whatever the cause or the reason, Brub and his management must have been doing a great many things right because 1949 turned out to be another record breaking year, with sales amounting to $5,453,000. The Company's net surplus had grown to $1,175,000.

As 1949 drew to a close, war was to enter the picture again. Management and many of the employees were concerned about the effect it would have on individuals and on the Company.

XXI More Mechanization
for Tree Service

U nder Brub's leadership the Company was experiencing the most dramatic growth in its entire history. Each year saw gains of a half million dollars and more, over the previous one. Based on this performance, management was very optimistic about 1950 . . . and beyond.

However, there was a cloud on the business horizon, which was a concern of both management and the employees of the Davey Company. It was the threat of war between North and South Korea, which promised to involve other nations as well.

The experience of World War II was still vivid in the minds of people who saw the Davey business shrink during that period. Also, there were a few who remembered the problems encountered during World War I. During both of those wars, the Davey Company had a struggle to keep alive.

Finally, in June of 1950, the Security Council of the United Nations asked member countries to help South Korea, which had been invaded by the North. The United States, along with fifteen other nations, agreed to send troops.

As a result, President Truman froze prices of all goods and services. By January of 1951, certain materials and products were rationed. However, before the Korean War began, and for several years following the end of World War II, Davey had been in the process of replacing trucks, sprayers and cars. In addition to replacements purchased during this period, the Company had expanded its ownership of equipment. Also, during the latter part of 1949 and in the early months of 1950, the Company had built up a substantial inventory of ropes, saws and other similar items necessary in carrying on field operations.

Line clearing had again been declared an essential activity. This meant the Company would be assured a substantial volume of business, and added another strength to carry on during the Korean War.

The growth of the Company during the previous several years had added to the financial reserves of the Company. At the end of 1949, the financial statement showed a surplus of $1,174,704: $94,000 in cash, the balance invested in equipment and inventory of parts and materials needed to carry on the business.

There was concern on the part of some of the directors about the amount of money tied up in equipment and inventory. This subject was explored in a Board meeting held in December of 1950. At that time there was a discussion about the advisability of paying a dividend. Paul Davey pointed out the difference between the period they were in and twenty years earlier, by stating, "The investment in equipment ties up our reserves and affects decisions, like paying dividends."

In response to Paul's remarks, Brub replied, "In 1951, if the manpower situation becomes a drastic one, the Company might have to depend on the revenues derived from the use of equipment and materials that will bring in money. If that is the case, we will be better off because we make more money on equipment, than on anything else we own."

In the ensuing discussion, Alexander M. Smith felt strongly that the Company should pay a dividend. After further debate, the rest of the directors agreed with him and voted a payout of five dollars per share.

The one imponderable, touched on in Brub's reply to Paul Davey, was manpower. How many men would the armed forces take? How many would be siphoned off into high paying defense industries? No one had any easy answers to these questions. It was a situation that was very difficult to evaluate. For instance, in August of 1950, there were more men in the Davey field force than there had been a year earlier. As it finally turned out, 200 Davey people were drawn into the armed services. Many of the salesmen and the foremen along with management did an excellent job of encouraging men to stay with the Company during the war instead of leaving for jobs in other industries.

Actually, the Korean War did not create a major disruption in the civilian economy. It was the first time that the United States supported both a war effort and a strong business activity on the home front. This effort was dubbed a "guns and butter economy." As a result, the Davey Tree Expert Company continued its phenomenal growth. Volume during

1950 rose to $5,864,000, an increase of more than $400,000 over 1949. In 1951 sales reached $6,722,000, 1952—$7,415,000 and in 1953, the last year of the war, they reached $8,359,000. The interesting aspect of these figures was that, unlike World War II when eighty percent of the volume came from line clearing, *all* of the services offered by the Company were showing healthy increases and contributed to the growing volume. Typical of the years to follow was the mix of 1951. In that year, Tree Care, which included Tree Surgery, Spraying, Mist Blowing and Tree Moving, amounted to $1,987,000; Chemical Brush Control reached $495,000; Line Clearing climbed to $4,239,000. A similar ratio evolved during the remaining Korean War Years.

During these years, even though there was some uneasiness on the part of a few people at the management level about the amount of money that was being invested in mechanical equipment, three new types of machinery were bought by the Company in and around the early Fifties. Ultimately, this new equipment was given an important role in the practice of Tree Surgery . . . and remains so to this very day.

One of the first of these new pieces of equipment was a Brush Chipper, introduced in the latter part of 1949. On any assignment where limbs and brush had to be removed, there was a problem of disposing of them. They were bulky and took time to properly load them onto a truck, then unload them at a suitable dumping ground which was becoming increasingly hard to find. When it was possible to do so, the best method was to burn the unwanted material however, that was not always permissible.

The Chipper helped to reduce the problem of disposing of limbs and brush. It is a machine which is towed behind a truck. Limbs and brush can be fed into it and the Chipper grinds them up and blows chips into a covered truck. It's a fast clean method, and of course, reduces the bulk tremendously. Also, the chips have some economic value because they are excellent mulching material. Initially two Chippers were bought and tested. Over the years an additional number were purchased and became an essential piece of field equipment.

Before the Chipper was introduced a number of ideas were used by the foremen to handle the removal of brush from the job site. Most of these dealt with methods of retaining the load on modified stake body trucks.

However, one of the foremen, Bryan Lindstrom, who was located in Valpariso, Indiana, built a piece of equipment which he used to dispose of brush. It consisted of a long, cylindrical furnace, which had insulated steel walls and a tall smokestack. Limbs and brush were fed into this fur-

Early brush chipper circa 1950.

nace and burned on the job site. The problem was that smoke, sparks and ashes escaped through the chimney. Because of this, on several occasions, he was faced with irate housewives who took a dim view of having ashes falling on freshly laundered clothes which had been hung out to dry.

Another piece of equipment introduced in 1953 was the Brush Hog which was a giant rotary mower hauled by a tractor. It chopped brush, including saplings up to three inches in diameter, leaving behind nearly pulverized material that was an excellent mulch. It was a very useful piece of equipment in mowing right-of-way and in special situations, such as along fence rows.

Probably one of the most spectacular pieces of equipment to be introduced about this same time was the Aerial Bucket. The first of these was bought by the Davey Tree Expert Company in December of 1953. The machine was equipped with an insulated boom to reduce the possibility of electrocution and had a Fiberglas bucket on the end. The machine was designed to lift two men forty feet from the ground. The equip-

170

ment was mounted on a truck. The boom could be rotated 360 degrees by controls located in the bucket.

The upper section of the boom was insulated with Fiberglas. The maximum load the Aerial Bucket could handle was 500 pounds. Fiberglas insulated pruners and other tools were pneumatically powered and were operated by throttles located on the handles. The air compressor which provided the power for the tools was mounted on the rear of the truck body.

When the truck was manuevered into the desired position, two steadying legs were lowered by push buttons located on the dash board of the truck. Also, on the dash was a switch for locking all of the wheel brakes while the boom was in operation.

Dean Ralph was in charge of the first Aerial Bucket. He and Arthur "Red" Emerick had been trained in its use by the manufacturer, located in Milford, Connecticut. This piece of equipment was especially adapted

Arthur "Red" Emerick in an early bucket truck in 1953.

to line clearing along streets and highways although it was used in other locations as well. One of the early uses of the Aerial Bucket by Davey was on the Fairlane estate, owned by Henry Ford, II, located in Dearborn, Michigan.

One of the important advantages offered by the Aerial Bucket was that it reduced the hazard of trimming trees close to high voltage power lines. When a man was working in that kind of location, he had to be extremely cautious and alert. Fortunately there were few accidents resulting from men coming in contact with high tension power lines. However, there were some. One of these resulted in Robert M. Ban, a Davey Tree Surgeon, receiving in 1950 the National Safety Council's President's medal. The award was given to Ban for saving the life of Slavin Soltesz on October 6, 1949. While sawing off a limb of a tree, Soltesz was overbalanced and thrown in contact with power lines carrying 440 volts. Ban lowered the unconscious Soltesz to the ground by a rope, then applied artificial respiration which was credited with saving the man's life.

Some years before, Austin E. Schneider, a Davey field supervisor, had been given the same award for saving the life of Harry Dickey, a member of his crew.

Because equipment was causing a major revolution in the way the Davey Tree Expert Company was operating, it is worthwhile to explore some of the reasons for this large investment. As labor costs increased it was necessary to increase the productivity of the field force. The volume of the Company had grown to such an extent that it was no longer possible to do all of the work with hand labor. Some of the services offered by the Company during this period, like spraying, tree moving and chemical brush control . . . just couldn't be done in any other way than through the use of mechanical equipment and be economically feasible.

As the Company expanded, it was constantly on the lookout for new growth markets. Sometimes this resulted in opportunities dictating the need for a specialized piece of equipment.

This was the case in 1949, when the sales department learned that the railroads had trouble clearing brush along their rights of way. This was immediately recognized as an excellent opportunity for Davey to expand the market for its Chemical Brush Control Service. But before the Company could enter the market, a new piece of equipment was needed so this was developed and used.

The spray unit built to meet the railroads' needs consisted of two vehicles equipped with flanged wheels, so they could ride along on the tracks. One unit was motorized and had a four-gun, sixty-gallon-per-minute sprayer mounted on it. The second unit was equipped with an auxiliary tank from which the sprayer could draw material without interrupting its operation. The equipment was first used in August of 1950 to clear brush along 200 miles of track in southern Ohio.

Many of the mechanical problems encountered in developing the railroad spray equipment were solved by Davey employees in the Kent, Ohio, shop.

While mechanization was of increasing importance to the Davey Tree Expert Company, a knowledge of human nature and the ability to deal with people was, and is, a very important quality in the operation of the tree business.

In many cases, before any kind of equipment could be used, or for that matter before any work could be done to clear power or phone lines, permission had to be secured from property owners to trim their trees. Permission was not always easy to get. Brub Davey likes to relate some stories about a man by the name of Vesta Jackson and the ways in which he overcame resistance from property owners in several difficult situations.

Vesta Jackson was a Will Rogers type and an excellent tree man. He knew trees and how to treat them and he was equally skilled in dealing with people. Because of this combination of skills, he was often used as a trouble shooter. One of his experiences dealt with a job for a utility company.

The assignment was secured through negotiations between top executives of the Davey Company and the utility company. As is usual in these kinds of situations, normal protocol was set aside, with the result that operating people became mildly upset, particularly in light of the fact that the assignment was to be a test to demonstrate that the Davey Tree Expert Company could clear lines faster and at less cost than the phone company could do it with its own men.

Naturally, after the agreement was made, details were turned over to operating people to carry out. The choice of the area in which Davey was to work was left to the men in charge of line clearing for the utility company. These company officials assigned the Davey crews to an in-town location, which meant a long, slow haul to get rid of the brush. But to add to the difficulty, tree owners in the area were irate because the last time tree trimming crews had worked in the neighborhood, trees had been badly butchered. This was hardly the ideal choice of a site to demonstrate the efficiency of Davey service.

A call went out for Vesta Jackson. After he arrived he sized up the problem and then worked out an approach to the property owners. He would go to the door of a home and say to the person who answered, "I am here to trim your trees. Where do you want me to put the brush?" By giving the people an immediate problem to solve, "where to put the brush," he avoided an argument about tree trimming, and by letting them decide how to dispose of the brush, he saved the Davey crews long, time-consuming and costly trips across town to a dump. Through this bit of strategy, Vesta Jackson was able to demonstrate the efficiency of Davey service.

Vesta's knowledge of human nature was shown in a couple of other instances. One time when he was approaching property owners for permission to trim their trees he walked up to a front porch and was surprised to see a man sitting there with a shotgun across his lap.

Vesta explained why he was there. The man then told him that the last people who trimmed his trees had messed them up. He then added that anyone who climbed his trees would be dropped with a load of buckshot.

Vesta stood there listening patiently until the man finished his tirade, and then he said, "That's a mighty fine gun you have there. You know when they made that gun they made another one just like it, and I own it, since there might be some shooting I think I'll go over to the house and get it."

With that he turned and started to leave, but before he got very far the man called him back and suggested that maybe they ought to talk things over.

Apparently the man was willing to start a war if he was the only one who was going to do the shooting. But if there was a possibility of someone shooting back, he was willing to negotiate a more reasonable solution, which was done. Vesta arranged it so the man could supervise the work so that no limbs would be removed from his trees without his permission.

In another case, Vesta was again calling on property owners for permission to trim their trees. Time-after-time people would say to him, "Go ahead and trim my trees, but I'll tell you something, that miserable old woman on the end of the street is never going to let you touch one of her trees."

Finally he reached the house of the woman with the forbidding reputation. He walked up to the front door and rang the bell. When the woman answered, he explained why he was there and closed by saying, "I guess I am just wasting my time because I've been told you won't let me touch one of your trees."

Very sharply she asked, "Who said that?"

He replied, "Almost everyone on the street said you're mean and unreasonable and will never let me trim your trees."

Almost before he finished, she said, "They said that? Well, those fools around here never know what they're talking about. You just go ahead, Mister, and trim my trees to your heart's content."

Knowledge of human nature was not confined to men in the field, like Vesta Jackson. Management also had this insight and exhibited it on many occasions in dealing with employees. Over the years there was recognition at the Davey Tree Company that people worked for more than wages. This understanding was revealed in September of 1951, at Brub's recommendation. Those in charge of field operations, sales, finance, office management, research and development were elected vice-presidents of the Company. This action was proof that Brub sincerely believed that all departments of the Company made important contributions to its total success.

Recognition of Davey's leadership in Chemical Brush Control, came about in January of 1951 when Homer L. Red Jacobs was the principal speaker at the Fifth Annual Meeting of The Northeastern Weed Control Conference. The meeting was held in the New Yorker Hotel in New York City. In attendance to hear Jacobs' paper were foresters, power and telephone men, staff members from federal and state experimental stations and representatives of several chemical companies. There were men there even from a number of Davey's competitors. In fact, men attended from practically every state from Massachusetts to the Carolinas. All were anxious to hear what the "Dean" of Chemical Weed Control had to say about the effectiveness of several chemicals in the Davey Company's highly successful weed control program.

In June of 1951, for the second time under Brub's management, the Group Insurance Plan was improved. Under the new plan, the Company paid sixty percent of the premiums. The previous plan called for the Company to pay 40% for groups, which included the field men, and a flat two dollars a month for all others. The new plan cost the Company twice the amount of the previous one. The benefits were also greatly improved. At the same time, the Company increased its share of the cost of the auto insurance carried by the foremen.

At about the same time, it was decided to put special emphasis on an area which had always received a great deal of attention from the Davey Company . . . safety. Almost from its inception, the Davey Bulletin carried articles on safety, or cartoons illustrating dangers to be avoided. Time and again it was stressed that an employee involved in an accident suffered not only pain, and worse, but an economic loss as well. From the Company's standpoint, safety was good business. Industrial insurance rates go up or down depending on the number and severity of accidents a company has. During 1951, the cost to Davey for this insurance was $165,000. Management was convinced that this figure could be cut in half, if everyone was safety minded. Toward this end, the Company ran a safety slogan contest. The winner was Asa H. Hubbell of Sarasota, Florida. His winning slogan was, "Make your Davey ways, safety ways." Safety has been a continuing, never ending program at the Davey Company.

In 1952 there were some changes made, dealing with the financial affairs of the Company. Up to that time some of the capital had been tied up in real estate needed in the operation of the business. Since this property was no longer needed it was sold. On the advice of the attorneys and brokers for the Davey Company, the proceeds from the sale of this property were invested in the common stocks of customers and suppliers. At the same time it was decided to begin a program of investing ten percent of the net profits (after taxes) in these same stocks. It was felt that this action would serve a definite business purpose. From 1952 to 1958, $257,-000 had been invested in this direction. The total gain on the investment for that period was $122,000.

By 1953 the Korean War had ended. Soon twenty-five of the men who had been in service rejoined the Company, to be followed shortly by another hundred who came back to resume their careers with Davey. These men returned to a much larger company . . . one whose volume had grown from $5,453,000 sales in 1949 to $8,359,000 in 1953, a gain of $2,906,000. This increase alone was larger . . . by almost a million dollars . . . than the total volume the Company was doing at the end of World War II.

But impressive as that record was, it was far from the end of growth and change. In fact, 1954 witnessed a very important event in Davey history. This was the year in which the building for the Davey Technical Service Center was completed. It is an attractive structure, forty-nine by sixty-three feet, located in Kent, Ohio.

The new building enabled management to put under one roof, the office, laboratory and library for the technical staff. There had also been provision made for adequate class rooms for students of the Davey Institute. In addition, the Technical Center housed the photographic department and its files of negatives, as well as the Davey Motion Picture Library. Also provision was made on the property for equipment storage and experimental plantings.

The first event in the new quarters was a supervisor's conference, held on December 15th and 16th of 1954. It was followed by the formal opening which took place two days later. Shortly after these events, a hundred officials of utility companies visited the Davey Technical Center for an open house, to provide them an opportunity to inspect the facilities. Attractive displays had been set up to demonstrate the wide scope of services Davey was able to offer. For the benefit of those in attendance, there were several demonstrations of new equipment like the chippers.

During this occasion, a number of the utility executives expressed their appreciation of Davey advertising. They pointed out that it created confidence among their customers in the skill of Davey Tree Surgeons. This helped when they had to approach home owners for permission to trim trees in order to clear power lines. They said owners felt better about granting approval when they knew the work would be done by Davey Tree Experts.

At the 1954 supervisors' meeting held at the Tech Center, "Biff" Staples introduced the group to a new type of speed saw developed by Davey employees. It cut faster and smoother than other types and was easier to sharpen because it did not require the use of a raker gauge to file it. On an ordinary saw, the raker teeth clears the sawdust from the cut which requires them to be set at a precise angle. Since the new speed saw did not have or need raker teeth the need for the gauge was eliminated, making sharpening easier and quicker. For many years, this

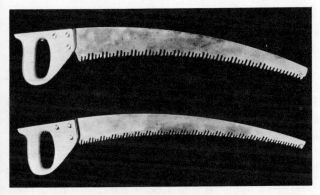

Top is a standard "speed" saw. Bottom an even faster cutting tool devleoped by a Davey saw designer.

saw was manufactured by the Atkins Saw Company, for the exclusive use of the Davey Tree Expert Company.

This investment in equipment was still being made at a substantial rate. At a Board meeting held in October of 1954, it was reported that a $217,000 investment had been made between January 1st and September 15th, in purchasing trucks, brush chippers, power saws, sprayers, circle saws and tractors.

While this was a very sizeable sum of money that had to come out of profits or borrowings, it pales in comparison to the amount of money paid to the employees in a typical year. In a 1954 discussion of this subject, it was pointed out that in the previous year, 1953, out of the total volume of $8,359,000 for the United States, $6,270,000 went to employees.

Regardless of what the figures showed, the Company needed people and it needed equipment. The trick was to wisely employ both so that the Company could grow and be profitable. And the Company did continue its forward thrust by establishing another new high for sales in 1954, reaching a total volume for the United States of $9,343,000.

One way that Davey was able to maintain its phenomenal growth was to encourage everyone to be a salesman for the Company. Toward this end, a series of articles appeared in the Davey Bulletin under the title of, "How to sell Davey Tree Service." There were a great many prospects for this service because the Company had a wide range of tree care services to offer in addition to the substantial volume the Company was doing in line clearing. These "other services," included spraying, pruning, tree feeding, lightning rod protection for trees, bracing, cabling, tree removal, tree planting, tree surgery, tree surveys . . . in fact everything having to do with general tree care.

While the Company was enjoying increased volume, unfortunately earnings did not keep pace with the growth. In 1955, Brub pointed out to his directors, that 1954 was the ninth consecutive year that the Company had shown substantial growth. The first eight months of 1955 were no different: at that point, sales were 6.1% over 1954. All services were showing substantial gains, except line clearing, which was up only one percent. Tree moving was up a hefty 60.74%.

He went on by saying, "In 1945 the earnings were seven percent. The years immediately following World War II, earnings, before profit sharing and taxes, were eleven to twelve percent. But in 1951 profit dropped to seven percent, in 1952 to six and a half, in 1953 to five and a half. Then in 1954 earnings rose to 8.85%. The 1955 forecast indicated earnings of 7½%. He pointed out that, "this was much too low." He also reminded the

Board that the last time the Company was out of the banks by December was in 1948. He proposed a real tightening of belts and a more cautious attitude in the purchase of mechanical equipment.

Brub felt that at least those important steps had to be taken if the Company was to improve its earnings performance. On the subject of new, heavy equipment, he said, "Before any purchase was made, the Company had to be sure it was going to get an adequate return on the investment."

There were, of course, some underlying causes for the decrease in earnings, the principal one being rising costs. The period from 1946 to 1955 witnessed some staggering increases in the cost of doing business. In that period, direct costs increased 150%; indirect charges skyrocketed 300%. The effect of all of this was that in 1955 the Company's net profit, after taxes and profit sharing, was a low 2.4%.

At the same time, the question was raised about the value of profit sharing as an employee incentive. After a rather lengthy discussion during which the pros and cons were carefully and thoroughly explored, it was decided to discontinue it after 1956.

Because profits were not at a satisfactory level, there were many others in the Company who shared Brub's concern about this area of the business. Many of them were trying to help solve the problem in one way or another. This is indicated by the positive suggestions which came out of a sales meeting in 1955.

One of the men, Billy White, expressed the opinion that tree moving had a greater potential than line clearing. He pointed out that a $25,000 to $30,000 house requires about a $1,000 worth of landscaping. He also said that landscaping of industrial buildings offered a good potential for profitable work and had the added advantage of being a suitable activity for the winter season. He was successful in developing work in these markets and offered his plans for others to use.

Lew Irvine, another of the men at the meeting, said that he found that high schools, colleges, golf courses, privately owned wooded lots and army and air force bases, were all good prospects for winter work. He agreed with White that industrial plants were very good prospects for tree moving.

There were others who offered ways in which business from the utilities could be increased. It was also brought out that pipeline companies, which were becoming of increasing importance at the time, offered possibilities as a new market for Davey services.

A lucrative source of business, was Davey Tree Food. It wasn't often discussed because it was over-shadowed by the more dramatic operations of the Company. It was an excellent product and a profitable one. In 1954, 1,098,501 pounds were sold. In fact special equipment had been developed to bore holes in the ground under the trees into which the fertilizer was poured and then capped with top soil or peat moss.

The proper feeding of trees adds to their beauty and value and trees do increase the value of a piece of property. Robert E. Marvin, a well known landscape architect at the time, estimated that a full grown shade tree was worth $1,000. He publicly urged owners to take care of their trees and to have the work done by the Davey Tree Expert Company and not by some "fly-by-night" outfit.

The interest and suggestions of the directors and the employees, is an indication that Brub did not stand alone in his concern for the welfare of the Company. He had a sympathetic Board of Directors and a responsive operating team. Both of these groups shared his desire to build a healthy, profitable volume for the Company.

By January of 1956 Brub had headed the Company just a few months less than ten years. It was time to pause and look back over the road where he had led the Company. It was a road that had passed over some rocky terrain . . . rising costs . . . a war . . . rapid growth . . . any one of these had the potential of creating serious problems if they were not handled with the greatest of care. It took intelligent, careful maneuvering to turn these into assets, and not permit them to become road blocks to success.

XXII 50 Years of Accomplishment

By now, after ten years of continuous and solid growth, that averaged almost half million dollars a year, the question might well have been asked, "To whom does the credit belong for the phenomenal growth of the Company?" If Brub were to answer, he would have promptly said, "The credit belongs to every person who works for the Davey Tree Expert Company. They are the ones who brought about success through their efforts." It would never have occurred to him to claim a major role in what was going on. Brub went to great lengths to give the people around him credit for the good things that were happening to the Company avoiding taking any credit for himself. In fact, there were times when he went too far in lavishing praise where it was not completely earned. However, he operated on the theory that if people received recognition for their efforts, even if they didn't always merit the praise, it buoyed their spirits and gave them an incentive to try harder.

It should also be told that Brub gave a great deal of credit to his father for much of the success the Company was enjoying. He has always been quick to point out that it was his father who laid the strong foundation under the Davey Company and that it was on this base the Company built its success.

Brub had no problem in sharing the glory for the growth which the Davey Company had experienced the previous ten years. But the record spoke for itself. It disproved the opinions expressed by those who had doubts when Brub, at age 28, took over the leadership of the Company. In reflecting on what actually happened with what might have been, if the doom sayers had been right, recalls a famous quotation which says, "Defeat is a bastard, but victory has a thousand fathers."

There were some fundamental differences in the business that had taken place since 1945, that called for different management techniques. For many years the largest single source of volume for the Davey Company came from large estates. Increased taxes, plus the higher costs of labor, made it almost impossible for these large estate owners to support their grounds, or to spend money on tree care as had been done in the past. As a result, the volume from that source greatly diminished. It was replaced by increased activity in line clearing and new services like chemical brush control and mist spraying. In addition to these newer services, the market had broadened to the point where thousands of individual home owners, industrial plants, cemeteries and golf courses were being served. By 1956 the business had grown to a much larger one than when Martin, Senior, was at the helm. While many of the principles and philosophy remained the same, the details of the business were so changed that it almost seemed like a completely different company. The times called for a different style of leadership. Brub was a delegator who not only charged people with the responsibility for running certain segments of the business, but also gave them the authority they needed to carry out their assignments.

An astute appraisal of Brub's leadership was made by Orrin B. Crosser, Vice-President for Finance. Crosser was a veteran of the Davey organization. He joined the Company in 1919, attended the Davey Institute, was editor of the Davey Bulletin, was Service Director for the Company and was elected Vice-President of Finance in 1951.

Crosser's remarks are taken from a report to the Company's employees entitled, "Ten Years of Progress," which appeared in the Davey Bulletin of April, 1956. In the report he said, "In any major projects taken under consideration by those of us who are active in management, we have at all times felt that we had the full support and backing of Mr. Davey whether we were trying to expand or retrench.

"We have felt free to make our decisions within the broad limits of Company policies, without any sense of being hampered or handcuffed to the point of inactivity.

"In other words, a business climate has been created within the Company in which the Management Committee has come to expect to be questioned about something that has not been done, rather than about something that has been accomplished. The questions put to us about a new project were; 'Is this a good or bad proposal?' 'If it's good, how can we afford it?' 'If we can afford it, how and when will it be paid for?' 'Where is the money coming from?' 'What kind of return can we expect from our investment?'

"Therefore, it seems fair to remark that a policy that has been described as being both conservative and aggressive has been both purposeful and effective for the Company. If this were not true, the annual statement of the Company might not look so well.

"Our President, during these past ten years has managed well by seeming to manage little and above all has been prudent and thrifty with human material."

Crosser's report also included some interesting financial data. He pointed out that the Company had experienced a tremendous growth in plant and equipment with money which had come from the business and not from outside investors. There were no encumbrances on the Company, such as bonds, long term loans or mortgages. The Company was free and clear, except for some short term loans which were more than offset by liquid assets such as life insurance and accounts receivable. Over 90% of them were as good as money in the bank.

A tabulation offered in Crosser's report revealed how much the cost of operating the business had increased in 1955 over 1946. The increased costs were due to inflationary pressures, improved employee benefits and a greatly expanded work force.

	1946	1955	Percent Increase
Sales	$4,000,000	$10,000,000	150%
Depreciation	41,000	217,000	429
Bldgs., Land, Equip. (Net)	385,000	1,074,000	179
Advertising	52,000	105,000	102
Research and School	27,000	47,000	74
Branch Offices	20,000	47,000	135
Office Supplies	40,000	80,000	100
Monthly Maintenance	6,000	14,000	133
Shops and Warehouses	36,000	97,000	170
Hand Tools, Equipment	67,000	113,000	69
Insurance:			
Industrial	93,000	227,000	144
General	29,000	65,000	125
Group	6,000	40,000	566
Co. Share, Foreman Equip.	—	15,000	—
Social Security Taxes	58,000	147,000	153
Federal Income Taxes	99,000	210,000	112
Other Miscellaneous Taxes	20,000	45,000	125
Interest Expense	5,000	21,000	320
Retirement	33,000	50,000	52

	1946	1955	Percent increase
Profit Sharing	66,000	100,000	52
Weekly Payroll	60,000	110,000	83
Materials, Supplies Inv.	67,000	137,000	105
Investments	——	104,000	——
Accounts Receivable	433,000	1,090,000	152

Note: For presentation purposes the figures in the table were listed in round numbers.

Volume had grown tremendously in these same years and while the sales figures for individual years have been presented earlier, it's interesting and revealing to look at the ten year record in its entirety.

Year	Tree Care— Including Tree Surgery Spraying, Mistblowing and Tree Moving	Brush Control	Line Clearing	Total
1946	$1,148,414.00		$2,757,872.00	$3,906,286.00
1947	1,257,656.00	$ 52,000.00	3,299,666.00	4,609,322.00
1948	1,397,183.00	271,463.00	3,559,306.00	5,227,952.00
1949	1,626,392.00	353,582.00	3,473,347.00	5,453,321.00
1950	1,762,879.00	411,877.00	3,688,839.00	5,863,595.00
1951	1,987,022.00	495,378.00	4,239,788.00	6,722,188.00
1952	1,998,833.00	659,902.00	4,755,881.00	7,414,616.00
1953	2,328,658.00	674,586.00	5,355,943.00	8,359,187.00
1954	2,746,602.00	621,436.00	5,975,060.00	9,343,098.00
1955	2,850,796.00	741,329.00	6,191,712.00	9,783,837.00

Note: The above figures do not include Canadian sales.

From the above it is easy to see the value Chemical Brush Control added to the Company after its inauguration in 1947. Mist Blowing was introduced in 1948, and was responsible for much of the increase shown in the Tree Care category. While both of these services made important contributions to income, they did require substantial investment in equipment.

In reviewing the previous ten years, Brub pointed out that it had been a decade of progress for the Davey Tree Expert Company. He offered a word of caution in connection with the report, by saying, "The review was not made or offered to lull the organization into a false sense of security." He stated further, "There is an important need for effort on the part of everyone to keep the Company strong so that it has the ability to keep moving forward."

While Brub had some concern that the ten-year review might make some people relax, he also felt that the review was important. He expressed his views on this subject in an article which appeared in the April, 1956, issue of the Davey Bulletin, in which he said, "I feel that everyone in the Davey Organization who had a part in the building program we have carried on over the past ten years should derive some feeling of satisfaction and pride in seeing what we have been able to do by working together." And by "working together" Brub and his team were able, in 1956, to produce the Company's first ten million dollar year.

In a discussion with the Board of Directors, dealing with the changes which had occurred in the business, Brub stated that, "It now takes $3,500 to put a three man crew in a tree." He continued by saying, "Formerly a foreman with a box of tools and a couple of men did the job. The men owned their own saws, chisels, mallets and slicks."

It is interesting to note that although the Company had gone through a revolutionary change in operating procedures, it continued to serve many clients for a great many years. For instance, a number of the utilities had been Davey clients for as long as twenty-eight years. Another effect that these changes created was that the ratio between quick assets and liabilities had shrunk during the past twenty years.

By 1957, the entire United States economy was starting to show some signs of softening. However, the Davey Company had plenty of work, enough at least to reach another high in volume, with sales of $10,761,336. But many of the Davey customers were suffering. As a result they refused to approve payments for overtime. This, in turn, reduced the income of the Davey field men. In concern for the men, Davey attempted to raise its hourly rates. But this met stiff resistance on the part of the clients. In fact, many of them reduced the amount of time Davey could work on their assignments in a week. This meant that expensive equipment had to stand idle reducing Davey profits, because equipment must be kept working if it is to be profitable.

By the following year, the depressed business economy caught up with Davey. As a result, for the first time since 1946 the Company showed a loss in sales volume by dropping to $10,223,000. Although the total sales for 1958 were down by five percent, some of the services were up substantially. Mist Spraying went from $142,841 in 1957 to $181,578 in 1958, a gain of twenty-seven percent. Winter tree surgery went from $214,154 to $259,679, a healthy increase of $45,525, regular tree surgery increased $64,669. The largest percentage of decrease was registered by Chemical Brush Control. It dropped nineteen percent, from $1,012,734 to $819,437. Line Clearing dropped $427,442. Although sales were down, the Company did show a profit of $337,183, about three and one-third cents per dollar of sales on a total volume of $10,223,000.

By the end of 1959 the Davey Company resumed its upward movement. Sales for that year jumped to $11,060,000. That, of course, was a new high for sales. But 1959 marked another important mile stone for the Davey Tree Expert Company . . . it marked the fiftieth anniversary of the Company's incorporation. It was on February fourth, 1909, that the Company was incorporated. The financial statement at the end of that first year listed Accounts Receivable at $19,243, tools and equipment (25% depreciated) $1,242. In comparison, at the beginning of 1959, Accounts Receivable were $1,160,945, Total invested in Buildings and Equipment (56% depreciated and not including land) $2,182,104, Net Book Value of buildings and equipment $960,506.

Another sharp contrast between the present and the past was offered in a report made to the stockholders on March 24, 1959, by Paul G. Hershey, who at the time was Vice-President for Field Operations. Part of his report included a list of equipment the Company owned in 1946 and what it owned at the end of 1958.

Equipment

Back in 1946, the Company owned
- 85 trucks
- 50 shade tree sprayers and
- 12 automobiles.

In checking our equipment inventory at the end of 1958 we owned
- 44 power wagons
- 10 skyworkers
- 311 trucks
- 247 power saws
- 10 tractors
- 56 circle saws
- 19 aerial ladders
- 20 automobiles
- 24 mist sprayers
- 132 brush chippers
- 73 shade tree sprayers
- 108 chemical brush sprayers
- 3 stump removers and
- 2 bulldozers

In addition to this, Davey leased during 1958
- 245 trucks from foremen
- 430 power saws from foremen

186

6 automobiles from employees
39 automobiles from a rental agency.

In the same report, Hershey made some comments about the Davey Institute, which had played such an important role in the history of the Company. He said, "We have a considerable amount of experience in the field today. The Davey Institute has graduated so many men since 1946 that it is getting to be a problem to find new qualified candidates. Last winter we had some difficulty getting enough men to fill our classes, because so many of the men in the field have had this advanced training." The remarks made by Paul Hershey underlined the changes the Company had gone through over the years. In recalling the history of the Davey Institute, it's remembered that when Martin, Senior, first opened this unique school, he paid a bonus to the men who were willing to attend. Later it became selective and a privilege to attend. And now in 1959 so many men had been trained, it was difficult to find suitable candidates. The changes experienced by the Davey Institute were a definite indication that the Company had reached maturity.

February 4, 1959 marked the fiftieth anniversary of the Davey Tree Expert Company as a corporate entity. It all started from an idea of a poor English immigrant, John Davey, who loved plants and trees. Out of that love welled the science of Tree Surgery which made it possible to protect and maintain the health of the trees he loved so much. He was the first to organize a text on shade tree care in his book "The Tree Doctor."

His son, Martin L. Davey a most unusual man, successful in business and politics made Tree Surgery a commercial success. In turn, his son, Martin L. Davey, Jr., built on that strong foundation a business that had assets of $2,500,000 when he took over in 1946 and in 1959 was worth $4,500,000.

The story of the Davey Tree Expert Company didn't end in 1959. In fact the Company has continued to prosper and grow and is alive and well today. Some idea of the subsequent success of the Company can be gathered from the fact that from 1970 to the end of 1974, sales rose $25,791,000 to $38,135,000.

During those rapidly growing years Alexander M. Smith, son-in-law of Martin L. Davey, was President of the Davey Tree Expert Company. The story of the struggles, covering the period from 1955 forward, will be left for another teller of tales to relate at some future time.

The purpose of this book was to relate the humble beginnings of an unusual company and its efforts to become a viable entity. It's a story that needed telling and many of the events needed to be preserved. But in the telling of the story, something else was revealed. . . . and that was, that the United States grew strong and developed the greatest economy the world has ever known because of the free enterprise system which allowed the Davey Tree Expert Company and thousands of other companies to rise from very modest beginnings to become large and successful enterprises. In that process unlimited opportunities were provided for the people of this great country. And that was the vision John Davey saw when he left England to seek his fortune in a new land.

Martin L. Davey, Jr., Milford "Biff" Staples

Index

311